MW00440726

EVERY PILGRIM'S GUIDE
TO ASSISI

Every Pilgrim's Guide to

ASSISI

AND OTHER FRANCISCAN PLACES

JUDITH DEAN

with illustrations by
Molly Dowell and Colin Dunn

PARACLETE PRESS
BREWSTER, MASSACHUSETTS

Every Pilgrim's Guide to Assisi and Other Franciscan Places

2006   First Printing

Text copyright © 2002 by Judith Dean
Illustrations copyright © 2002 by Molly Dowell and Colin Dunn

ISBN 1-55725-514-8

This edition published by Paraclete Press, 2006.
Originally published 2002 in the United Kingdom under the title
Every Pilgrim's Guide to Assisi by the Canterbury Press Norwich
of 9-17 St. Albans Place, London N1 0NX

Acknowledgments:
The Prayers of St. Francis, compiled by W. Bader,
New City Press, 1986 (used by permission).
Praying with Clare of Assisi, by Ramonia Miller,
St. Mary's Press, 1994 (used by permission of the publisher).
All rights reserved.
I also wish to thank Molly Dowell and Colin Dunn
for their superb illustrations.

Library of Congress Cataloging-in-Publication Data
Dean, Judith, 1959-
  Every pilgrim's guide to Assisi and other Franciscan places / Judith
Dean ; with illustrations by Molly Dowell and Colin Dunn.
    p. cm.
Originally published: Norwich : Canterbury Press, 2002.
Includes bibliographical references and index.
ISBN 1-55725-514-8
1. Assisi (Italy)--Guidebooks. 2. Church buildings--Italy--Assisi--
Guidebooks. 3. Francis, of Assisi, Saint, 1182-1226--Shrines.
4. Italy--Guidebooks. I. Title.
  DG975.A8D4 2006
  914.5'651--dc22   2006021013

Typeset by Rowland Phototypesetting Ltd.

Published by Paraclete Press
Brewster, Massachusetts
www.paracletepress.com

Printed in the United States of America

Contents

Contents

Preface

In September 1997, television screens worldwide showed
scenes of a small historic town in central Italy hit by an
earthquake. The reason why Assisi received so much
attention was only in part due to the magnificence of its
architecture or its scenic location. St Francis is without
doubt one of the best-known saints and news of the damage
to the basilica built in his honour, saddened and shocked
Christians and non-Christians alike, such is the appeal of
the 'poor man of Assisi'.

Today, due to the remarkable efforts of the citizens of
Assisi, specialists and much outside support, most of Assisi
looks more splendid than ever and is welcoming pilgrims
again as it has for centuries. However, it is not the buildings
that most visitors comment on, whatever their reasons for
coming here, but the unique atmosphere of the town which
allows everyone regardless of their faith or beliefs the space
in which to calmly reflect surrounded by such a stunning
natural setting. Francis with his deep love of all creation
offers hope and inspiration for all, which accounts for Pope
John Paul II inviting heads of other faiths to Assisi to
consider the role that all religions have to play in bringing
about peace in the world.

This book does not offer a detailed biography of the
saint's life or a comprehensive travelogue of this area.
Instead here is a practical guide, providing an introduction
for those wishing to discover more about Francis, Clare and
the lands where they lived and spread the gospel message.

I have included a short Glossary at the back of the book.
It gives brief explanations of some technical terms used.

Practical Information
for Travellers

Author's Note

The general information about opening times and facilities was accurate at the time of writing but is subject to change and, therefore, should be used as a guide only.

Bank Holidays

It is important to be aware of the dates of bank holidays otherwise they can spoil your plans because musems and monuments can be closed or have Sunday opening times.

National holidays in Italy are:

1 and 6 January
Easter Monday
25 April (Liberation Day)
1 May (Labour Day)
15 August (Ferragosto – the Assumption)
1 November (All Saints Day)
8 December (Immaculate Conception)
25–26 December

Bars, Cafés and Restaurants

You will never struggle to find a cup of coffee while on your travels in Italy as almost every town and village will have its own bar if not a restaurant or two. Bars are generally open from early in the morning to late at night and even on Sundays, but you will find that both bars and restaurants close *per turno*, in other words they will have a different day of the week when they are closed to ensure that there is always somewhere open, but this will be shown on the door. Bars, do not, as their name suggests, serve just alcoholic drinks. Far from it, as this is the place the Italians take their regular coffee fix, but come in too for a pre-lunch or dinner aperitif. This is also the place for a snack, sandwiches, rolls, cakes and maybe hot dishes at lunchtime accompanied by a variety of drinks: hot, cold, alcoholic and soft. Italian coffee needs a little explanation otherwise you might not receive what you thought you had ordered.

Caffè is just pure coffee made with very little water – what we would call espresso.

Caffe Americano is *caffe* with a lot of water added akin to what we
    might call a filter coffee (black).
Cappuccino is coffee with frothy milk added on top.
Caffe Latte served in a tall glass is coffee with a lot of hot milk on
    top.
Tea will be served without milk, so if you want it make sure you ask
    for 'tè con latte'.

Restaurants are generally open at lunch (12.30–3.00pm) and dinner
(7.00–10.30pm) and usually closed one day a week. It is not often
that you find restaurants open all day and self-service is only a
feature of bigger tourist centres and cities. It is becoming more
accepted now in Italy to take just one or two courses rather than the
whole affair and it is quite common to find either a tourist menu or
a set menu of the day. Pizzerias are found everywhere and have
similar opening times to restaurants. In general prices are quite
reasonable compared to eating out in England which is in part due
to the low cost of wine in Italy, but the quality is also comparatively
high as long as you avoid the obviously tourist-orientated
establishments.

Climate

Spring (April–June) is usually a good time to visit central Italy as
although the beginning of April can be wet, temperatures soon rise
and 70°F is not uncommon. May and June are almost always fine,
it being rare to experience anything that we would consider cold
and much more likely to be quite warm enough, reaching 80°F by
the end of June.

    Summer (July–mid-September) is often very hot by British
standards which accounts for the long school holiday in Italy.
Temperatures in the 90's are normal at midday, with the risk of a
storm breaking in the afternoon. Mosquitoes are fairly frequent
visitors to these parts during the summer, so precautions should be
taken in the evening and at night.

    Autumn (late September–November) is an opportune time to
visit this area as it is generally still warm, approx. 65°F–75°F and
for the most part dry (although rain can be a feature of November
weather). It is also scenically beautiful with the changing colours of
the landscapes.

    Winter (December–March) is changeable! You could be lucky
and have very temperate weather and sunny days, but on the other
hand it could be cold and wet. Generally, Umbria does not suffer
much in the way of cold snaps except for every ten to fifteen years
when the snowfall can be quite heavy. Advantages of visiting in
winter are that places are much quieter, easier to visit and that the
countryside never appears very bleak as it is mainly semi-
coniferous, so looks verdant even at this time.

Clothing

Only one thing is important about clothing when touring –
comfort, especially shoes. Umbria is far from flat and the streets
within the towns are often cobbled or ancient, so quite uneven.
Visitors are expected to dress respectfully when going into
churches no matter what the temperature is outside and this means
women covering shoulders and avoiding very short skirts and men
wearing a shirt and not donning skimpy shorts. This dress code can
be vigorously applied for the more visited churches where there is
an attendant and there is no question of being admitted until you
have adjusted your apparel to meet his approval!

Don't forget that towns like Assisi are situated at altitude and
will feel cooler in the morning and evening, so a light jacket will be
needed even in the hottest months.

Currency

As from 28 February 2002 the lira ceased to be legal tender and the
euro is now the currency of Italy, with five, two and one hundred,
fifty, twenty, ten and five euro notes and one, two, five, ten, twenty
and fifty cent (centestimi) coins as well as coins worth one and two
euros. The euro rate hovers at 60 to 65 pence sterling.

It is advisable to take some euros with you to cover immediate
expenses but sensible either to take travellers cheques for the rest of
your requirements or make use of the cash dispensers that you will
find in any town no matter how small and which offer a good rate of
exchange and are accessible with most high street bank cards. If
you are taking travellers cheques it is wise to remember that banks
are open in the morning 8.30am–1.00pm, they will only reopen for
an hour in the afternoon 3–4pm or 4–5pm and transactions can
take their time as you normally have to queue twice, for the paper
work and to receive the money. In larger or tourist towns like Assisi
it is better to find a bureau de change, but here or at a bank proof of
identity is a must.

Credit cards are now officially accepted in many places but cash
is often preferred especially for small items and it is worth bearing
in mind that a 'sconto' (discount) is more likely to be given if
paying in cash. It is always a good idea to check before you eat or
buy that credit cards are accepted and that you have some ready
money just in case.

Electrical appliances

Electrical current in Italy is 220V AC with two-pin, round-
pronged plugs which means that you will need an adaptor.
Many hotels do not allow customers to use electric kettles or
irons in the rooms, so do take note of any relevant notices to this
effect.

Health

Italy is covered under the reciprocal health agreement of the EU and so you should obtain and complete the E111 form from your local post office, making sure that you take it with you on holiday. You are entitled to free treatment but you will need to pay the bill first and then be reimbursed from the relevant government office. As this is not always convenient when you are on a short trip it is advisable to take out health insurance because this will also take care of any costs involved in repatriation or convalescence as well as covering you for loss or theft of goods.

The telephone number for the emergency services is 113. For minor ailments it is worth remembering that a chemist's (*farmacia*) in Italy is allowed to sell antibiotics and other medicines without a prescription and the pharmacist is a good source of advice. If you require treatment urgently for more serious problems, then you will need to find your way to a Pronto Soccorso (equivalent of an accident and emergency department).

Meals

Breakfast hardly features as a meal for most Italians being merely some coffee and bread or a pastry and this is still the most usual thing to be served in a modest hotel or religious guesthouse with the addition of some fruit juice, if you're lucky. Be warned that tea is not automatically served with milk in Italy or made with boiling water (sometimes just hot). In more expensive hotels you will probably find the above supplemented with cold meats, yoghurt, cake and fruit.

Lunch and Dinner are still traditionally eaten at home, lunch at about 1.00pm and dinner from 8.00pm (although hotels will often serve groups from 7.00pm). Both meals can have four courses but none is meant to be large and the main course is not as large a portion as in a typical British meal. The traditional order of a meal is:

Antipasto starter; *Primo* a pasta or rice dish; *Secondo* meat, fish or cheese with which you can eat *contorni* (vegetables), but note that they are not compulsory as in English cuisine and it is common just to have one. *Dolce* pudding/sweet, which can often be fruit.

Coffee is not always offered after a meal in a restaurant or hotel but this is becoming more common although Italians will still go to a café after dinner. Butter is served with bread for breakfast but not at lunch or dinner.

Passports

Anyone travelling from the UK will need a full ten-year passport, but from other EU countries a national ID card will suffice. For visitors from outside the EU visas are not necessary for US, Canadian and Australian citizens but other nationalities should seek advice from the Italian Embassy (Visa Section).

Security

Wherever there are tourists there will be someone waiting to take advantage of their generosity, often unbeknown to the donor! Organized groups of what often seem very young people operate in many Italian towns, as they do all over Europe and are very skilled at taking your possessions from you when you are at your most relaxed and least suspecting. There are of course hotspots such as around the Trevi Fountain and Colosseum in Rome, but pickpocketing can happen anywhere and so the answer is to take precautions:

• Only take with you what you really need for the day and leave the rest of your valuables in the hotel safe.
• Don't put wallets or purses in obvious pockets such as in the back of trousers.
• Don't take your passport with you, a photocopy will normally suffice for gaining reductions for museum entrances, etc.
• Handbags should be worn across the body not over the shoulder.
• Keep any bags or possessions close to you when you are in a café or sitting in a public place, preferably with straps secured around the chair leg.
• Bury purses and credit cards at the bottom of your bag, making them hard to access.

These warnings may sound offputting but if precautions are taken then you will not be troubled and will avoid an incident that could spoil your holiday. Travel insurance is recommended in case you should lose anything or have it stolen.

Shopping

Many people find shops in Italy a refreshing change after the large chain and department stores in Britain, as the shopping and commercial centres have not really arrived here yet. Small shops dedicated to a certain product are still the rule even in large towns and cities in Italy which make browsing more pleasant and buying more of a temptation. Craft shops are quite common and cake shops (*pasticcerie*) selling homemade cakes and sweets often of a regional variety are commonplace.

Generally shops will be open from 9.00 or 9.30 in the morning until 1.00pm and then from 3.00 or 4.00pm until 7.30pm. Shops are open on Saturdays (and some on Sunday mornings), but generally closed on Monday mornings.

Telephones

The days of having to use tokens in a public phone box are over as telephone cards (*scheda telefonica*) are available in different denominations and you can easily call home from a kiosk, although in some towns you will still find the central office where an operator will connect you and you pay afterwards. The code for Britain is 00 44 followed by the town code minus the '0' at the beginning.

Time

Italian time is one hour ahead of British time and clocks go forward and back at the same time as in England.

Tipping

Service is included by law in restaurant prices therefore only a small tip is necessary and likewise in bars. In hotels tipping is not expected and therefore at the customer's discretion. Tips are generally much appreciated whatever is offered, but in very touristy areas you may feel under more pressure to leave a sizeable sum!

General note: Opening times were correct at the time of going to press, but are liable to seasonal variation and change.

A Brief Biography of St Francis

This short desciption of Francis' life is little more than a chronology and serves only as a guide to the order in which events in the saint's life occurred, for a more detailed and helpful biography readers should consult any one of the many good works that have been written.

1182 (1181?)	Francis is born in Assisi to Madonna Pica and Pietro di Bernadone, a cloth merchant of the middle (minores) class. He is baptized in San Rufino cathedral and then receives basic schooling at the school held in San Giorgio chapel (part of St Clare's Basilica today). He undoubtedly is trained by his father to follow him in the cloth trade and probably accompanied him to France.
1202 –03	Francis joins the army of Assisi in battle against the city of Perugia but is taken prisoner after Assisi is defeated and he spends about a year in prison in Perugia after which he returns to his home a sick and changed man.
1203 –08	Francis, dissatisfied with life, takes to roaming the countryside in order to decide how to pursue his future. Illness thwarts his attempt at becoming a great knight, he hears the voice from the crucifix in San Damiano telling him to 'Repair my church' which is the start of his mission to follow the call of Christ. Francis rejects his father's demands and seeks a life of total simplicity to which others are soon attracted. Francis has his vocation confirmed by the gospel reading in Santa Maria degli Angeli, one of the churches he repairs.
1209	Pope Innocent III gives verbal approval of Francis' small band of brothers known as 'Friars Minor' and they make the chapel of the Porziuncula at Santa Maria degli Angeli their centre.
1212	Francis receives Clare at San Damiano and clothes her in the habit, marking the foundation of the second Franciscan order.

1212   At Alviano Francis draws up a rule of living for lay people, thereby marking the inception of the Third Order of Franciscans.

1219 –20   Francis journeys to the Holy Land in order to try and stop the crusade and en route meets and impresses the Sultan of Egypt.

1221   Francis presents the first version of the written Rule for the order at the General Chapter.

1223   The Rule is finally revised at Fonte Colombo and Francis undergoes treatment for his eye condition. At Christmas, Greccio witnesses the first live nativity representation, organized by Francis.

1224   Francis receives the stigmata (the wounds of Christ) at La Verna.

1226   Francis dies in the Porziuncula on the evening of 3 October and is buried in San Giorgio chapel.

1228   Pope Gregory IX proclaims Francis a saint and in 1230 his body is transferred to the newly built basilica.

1939   Francis is declared patron saint of Italy jointly with Catherine of Siena.

1979   Pope John Paul II declares St Francis the patron saint of ecology.

A Brief Biography of St Clare

| 1194? | Clare (Chiara) is born into the noble family of Offreduccio in the area occupied by the 'maiores' (upper) class near to the cathedral of San Rufino. |

| 1200 | Civil unrest in Assisi causes the Offreduccio and other noble families to take refuge in Perugia but they return after Assisi is defeated in battle by Perugia in 1202. |

| 1211 | Clare meets Francis for the first time and is so impressed that she is determined to follow a life of poverty like his. |

| 1212 | After attending the Palm Sunday celebrations in San Rufino, Clare leaves her home and Francis presents her with a habit. Clare lives in two women's religious communities before settling at San Damiano and is followed here by her sister, Caterina, who takes the name of Agnes.

Francis sets down guidelines for Clare's community, known as the 'Form of Life'. Clare accepts the title of Abbess of San Damiano and Pope Innocent III agrees to allowing Clare and her sisters to have the 'Privilege of Poverty'. |

| 1224 –26 | Beginning of Clare's long illness. During his stay at San Damiano, Francis composes the 'Canticle of the Creatures'. Clare's mother, Ortolana, follows her daughters into the convent at San Damiano. Francis dies on 3 October 1226 and Pope Gregory entrusts the care of the Poor Clares to the Friars Minor, at the same time renewing the Privilege of Poverty. |

| 1229 | Clare's sister Beatrice also joins the community at San Damiano. |

| 1240 | San Damiano is surrounded by Saracen forces under the command of the emperor but they leave peacefully after they see Clare carrying the monstrance containing the consecrated host. |

1247   Clare starts to compose a Rule for her community
–50   after Pope Innocent IV issues a general Rule for
        Poor Ladies.
            Clare's illness worsens.

1253   Pope Innocent IV twice visits San Damiano and
        Clare finally recieves confirmation of her Rule on
        her deathbed and she dies on 11 August. The pope
        attends her funeral in the chapel of San Giorgio in
        Assisi.

1255   Clare is canonized on 15 August by Pope Alexander
        IV at Anagni.

1260   The Poor Clares move into their newly built
        convent and the body of St Clare is placed in the
        basilica.

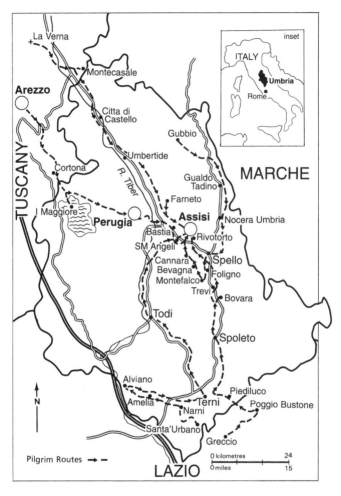

Franciscan Itineraries in Umbria and Tuscany

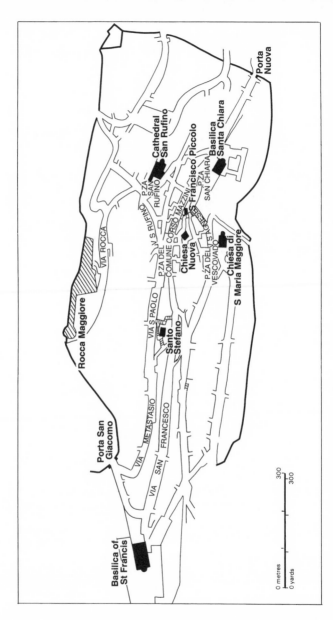

Plan of Assisi

Assisi: In the Footsteps of St Francis

Piazza Comune – Chiesa Nuova – San Francesco Piccolo –
San Rufino – Santa Chiara – Piazza Comune

Suggested time for this itinerary – half a day.

It is always tempting to start a tour of Assisi by visiting the
Basilica of St Francis, which so dominates the view of the
city as you approach it from the plain below. However, to
start there is to begin at the end, this is Francis' final resting
place and somewhere unknown to him during his lifetime. In
addition the basilica shows us what others thought of Francis
but does not tell us of his life or how he came to be considered
a saint. A more rewarding approach to unlocking the heart of
this beautiful place is to discover the city as Francis would
have known it and see the places that can tell us about him
and the world he lived in.

CHIESA NUOVA

Access

From the Piazza Comune
with the Roman temple
(Church of Santa Maria sopra
Minerva) on your left take the
small street at the top right-
hand corner of the square
which leads down to a small
square in which is the Chiesa
Nuova church. Please note that
there are some stairs to climb
up and down through the
church to see the area which
occupies what was Francis'
home and his father's business
premises.

History

The name 'Chiesa Nuova'
denotes that this church was
new (by Assisi standards!) and
only built in the seventeenth

century to make more
permanent one of the sites
associated with the life of St
Francis. The church was built
over what many believe to have
been where the property of
Pietro di Bernadone (Francis'
father) was located. Pietro was
an affluent cloth merchant and
would have possessed a
complex of shop and living
accommodation and here St
Francis was born and raised
until the age of twenty, when he
went to war on the side of
Assisi against the nearby city of
Perugia.

Tour

Pause a moment outside the
church and note the modern
bronze statue of Pietro di
Bernadone and Mona Pica,
Francis' parents. Mona Pica is

carrying broken chains, the significance of this is explained below.

Go inside the church and on your left you will see the 'cell', a stone enclosure with a metal grate. By tradition it is here that Francis' father locked him up after he had started to live a life of poverty instead of following in Pietro's trade and was being proclaimed by many in Assisi as a mad man. Mona Pica, his mother, was more indulgent and when asked what her son would become had replied, 'through grace he will become a son of God'. Of course she let him out of his prison, hence the broken chains on the statue outside.

To the left of the altar you will see a door marked 'santuario', go through this and you enter an area which reveals more of the Bernadone lodgings and enterprise. Although the lay-out of these buildings may seem unclear, the extent of the premises gives some idea of the reasonable wealth of the family and the prominent place it occupied in Assisi society. Here the cloth that Pietro had brought back from his trips within Italy and into southern France would have been stored and sold, which had given him a taste for French style and culture also adopted by his son. It is likely that there was also some cloth dying taking place here employing several people and so these rooms would have been a hive of activity.

One of the rooms has been converted into a small oratory which is a convenient palce to sit for a few minutes and perhaps consider what the *Legend of Three Companions* (a contemporary account of his life) tells us of those early days in Francis' life:

Francis grew up quick and clever and he followed in his father's footsteps by becoming a merchant. In business, however, he was very different from Pietro, being far more high-spirited and open-handed. He was also intent on games and songs; and day and night he roamed about the city of Assisi with companions of his own age. He was a spend-thrift and all that he earned went into eating and carousing with friends. His parents remonstrated with him, saying that in squandering such large sums on himself and others made him appear not so much their son as the son of a great prince.

You leave the church by a narrow passageway which was a street in medieval Assisi not a deserted alley and as you leave remember that this complex that now seems a redundant shell was then at the centre of the commercial and social hub of the city.

SAN FRANCESCO PICCOLO

Access

From the exit of the Chiesa Nuova complex turn right and at the end of this narrow street

San Francesco Piccolo

opposite you will see the oratory of San Francesco Piccolo.

Details

Standing outside you will see ranged around the doorway the Latin words: 'Hoc oratorium fuit bovis et asini stabilium in quo natis est sanctus Franciscus mundi speculum'. ('This oratory was the stable where Francis, mirror of the world, was born'.)

This place has been known as the Oratory of St Francis since the Middle Ages and therefore, it seems reasonably likely that this site was part of Bernadone family property. Tradition has it that this was a stable and like Mary, Christ's mother, Mona Pica gave birth to her son in an animal shelter. Fiction or not, the point of the story is as important now as to pilgrims in the thirteenth century, that Francis' life was modelled on that of Jesus and he lived up to that name given to him by his contemporaries of 'alter Christus' – the other Christ.

The simplicity of the oratory's interior accords well with the spirit of Francis' life and is a good place to reflect on Francis' joy in a life of total poverty.

SAN RUFINO

Access

From San Francesco Piccolo trace your steps back to the main square (Piazza Comune) and from there take the Via S. Rufino in the top left-hand corner uphill. The incline is quite steep but taken at a gentle pace is not too severe and once in the piazza of S Rufino you are on the level.

History

It would be natural to think looking at the skyline of Assisi that the Basilica of Assisi, standing astride the slope of Monte Subasio and dominating one's first view of the city, must be the cathedral. However, there had been a cathedral in this town for hundreds of years before Francis was born and at the time of his birth in 1182 San Rufino had been the cathedral for nearly 150 years. The cathedral is dedicated to San Rufino, the first Christian Bishop of Assisi, martyred for his faith by the Romans in AD 238 by being drowned in the river Chiascio which flows in the valley below Assisi. Rufino's body is buried under the high altar. It was to this cathedral that both St Francis and St Clare were brought to be baptized.

Tour

Exterior of the cathedral

Stand in the piazza for a few minutes prior to entering the church and look at the surrounding buildings, these are some of the oldest in Assisi and were within the quarter of the city occupied by the 'maiores', the nobility. Chiara (Clare) di Favarone d'Offreduccio was born into this class and the location of her family home can be seen next to the cathedral on the left as you face it, which is confirmed by the plaque on the wall.

Note also the façade of the church, this is one of the masterpieces of Romanesque architecture in Umbria and is a riot of exquisitely carved figures mythical and biblical. Around the beautiful rose window are the four animals which represent the evangelists and at the entrance there are two crouching lions, one devouring a man and the other holding a man in his claws, these beasts are meant to put you in a sombre frame of mind before entering the cathedral! It is worth mentioning that during Francis' lifetime the construction of this cathedral was in progress, as the previous one had been torn down to make way for an up-to-date model which was finally finished in 1253.

Interior of the cathedral

Entering the cathedral, your first thought is possibly that the interior is an anti-climax after the magnificent exterior and this is due to changes carried out in the sixteenth century because the building was showing signs of severe structural stress. In spite of this we can still see the font where both Francis and Clare were baptized, by going to the far right-hand corner of the church as you enter it. It was to this font that Francis' mother brought him to be baptized, as by all accounts his father was

away on business at the time of his birth and it was normal then for babies to be baptized straightaway because of the high risk of infant death. Contemporary sources record that Mona Pica named him Giovanni (John) but that Pietro, on his return, decided it should be changed to 'Francesco'. This was an odd choice as Francesco was not a recognized name at the time and broke with the tradition of taking a saint's name or being called after a member of the family, as it merely means a French man. Doubtless the name Francesco was inspired in part by Pietro's visits to France but perhaps also from a desire to outdo his peers.

San Rufino played an important part in St Clare's life some time after her baptism when she was eighteen years old and came to the cathedral for the mass of Palm Sunday. Clare was in turmoil because she had secretly decided to leave her family and follow Francis and so did not move from her place for the blessing of the palms, but the priest came to her all the same and placed a palm in her hands. This was taken by Clare to be a sign encouraging her to embark on her radical choice.

Before leaving San Rufino go to the left of the main door where in a recess you will see a relic of Assisi's ancient past, a Roman cistern and part of the wall at this point is also from the same period.

Francis had a great respect

5

for the traditions and heritage of the church and exhorted all his disciples to do the same in a prayer he dictated on the last day of his life and this serves as a very fitting reflection to say in this or any church we enter on our travels:

> *We adore you,*
> *Lord Jesus Christ,*
> *in all the churches*
> *throughout the whole world*
> *and we bless you,*
> *because by your holy cross*
> *you have redeemed the world.*

If time permits you may like to visit the cathedral museum (small entrance charge), which contains frescoes and other works taken from various religious buildings in Assisi as well as the third-century sarcophagus of San Rufino. The museum can be reached through a door in the wall of the piazza, to the right as you face the cathedral.

BASILICA OF ST CLARE

Access

From San Rufino, take the sharp left turn following the wall of the cathedral downhill, round the bend to the right. At the road junction turn left, then a little way along turn right down to the Basilica of Santa Chiara (St Clare), and at the end turn right to reach the Piazza and main door.

History

Where you are standing now lay outside the city walls at the time of Francis but shortly afterwards this area became urbanized and the great gate which ends the street on which the basilica stands is called 'Porta Nuova' (the new gate) even though it was constructed in the fourteenth century!

Francis would have only known part of the present church, which is the right-hand section appearing as an extension because it is not built from the same striped stone as the rest. This was the chapel of San Giorgio which served as both a hospital and a school run by the canons of San Rufino and it was here that Francis received a rudimentary education, learning to read and write but probably little else as we know that he wrote in his native Italian dialect rather than Latin. It was also in this chapel that Francis gave his first sermon and in the crypt that his body was placed and maintained until he was canonized and the new Basilica of St Francis was finished. The major part of the church was built between 1257 and 1265 to house the tomb of St Clare who died in 1253.

Exterior

The piazza in front of the basilica was built in the nineteenth century and is like a terrace affording some of the best views of the city and the surrounding area. If you have your back towards the balustrade and open countryside you can see not only San Rufino where you

View towards the Basilica of St Clare

have just walked from but also above that the remains of the great medieval fortress, Rocca Maggiore. Turning round and to your right below you, you see the apse of the church of Santa Maria Maggiore (first cathedral of Assisi) and you can now appreciate the Roman method of town planning on stepped levels, which was adopted in the centuries that followed.

The positioning of the Basilica of St Clare was not entirely haphazard as it almost faces the Basilica of St Francis at the opposite end of the city and being of a similar design to the Upper Basilica of St Francis it seems to create a symbolic balance, the two great saints of Assisi watching over and supporting the town of their birth.

Interior

(Numbers in brackets refer to those on the plan)
Enter the basilica by the front door and the first impression is of a dark empty interior but it needs closer inspection to discover corners which reveal something of both St Francis and St Clare. Proceed up the main aisle and look at the chapel (1) on your left, this is dedicated to St Agnes, not the Roman martyr but Clare's own sister. Such was the attraction of the community Clare started at San Damiano that not only her sister but her mother, Ortolana, and other relatives and friends joined her too. Agnes is buried under the altar in this chapel. Frescoes here

juxtapose incidents from the life of Christ with that of Clare.

The large cross suspended above the main altar (2) is late thirteenth century and was commissioned by the then abbess who is depicted at the base of the cross along with St Francis and St Clare. If you continue down the right-hand side of the nave you will find a chapel (3) that contained the former Chapel of San Giorgio. (This area has been restructured recently and photographs taken before the 1997 earthquake will show two chapels here.) Hanging above the altar is a twelfth-century cross showing a typical representation of that period but this cross is special for its association with St Francis. It was in front of this crucifix that Francis prayed when it hung in the small church of San Damiano, during the time in his early twenties when he did not know the direction his life should take and wandered around Assisi waiting for inspiration. It was from this cross that he felt God had spoken to him this message: 'Do you not see that my house is falling into ruins? Go then and repair it for me.'

Francis took this demand literally and began his campaign that marked the beginning of a life spent faithfully carrying out Christ's will. It is very appropriate to pause here and say Francis' own prayer as recorded he said in reply to God's request.

Basilica of
St Clare

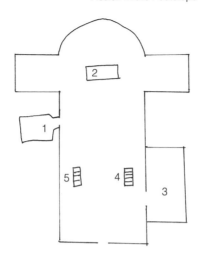

1 Chapel of St. Agnes
2 High Altar
3 Chapel of San Giorgio (Chapel of the Crucifix)
4 Entrance to crypt
5 Exit from crypt

Most high and glorious God,
enlighten the darkness of my
*   heart*
and give me sound faith,
firm hope and perfect love.
Let me, Lord, have the right
*   feelings*
and knowledge,
properly to carry out
the task that you have given
*   me.*

The crucifix was brought up to
the chapel of San Giorgio when
the community of Poor Clares
from San Damiano moved here
after Clare's death and has been
safeguarded by them ever since.
Attending daily evening mass
here is a serene experience
offering an ideal opportunity to

contemplate the crucifix and its
message.

Crypt

After leaving the Chapel of the
Crucifix, go down the stairs
nearby (4) into the crypt to see
St Clare's tomb. Clare died in
1253 in San Damiano but the
sisters moved from there once
they had negotiated with the
canons of San Rufino to occupy
San Giorgio, as San Damiano
was too isolated and vulnerable.
Her body was buried in the
place facing you as you reach
the bottom of the stairs, which
you can climb up to see better.
At the time of her burial there
was no access or chapel as
there is today, this was all

created when an excavation was carried out in 1850 to prove that the body was really there. The remains of Clare, being found incorrupt, were placed in the glass case that you now see but were covered by the casing some years ago as the process of decay set in.

Around the sides of the chapel are a series of photographic reproductions of monochrome drawings of the life of Clare.

PIAZZA COMUNE

Access

From Piazza Santa Chiara with your back to the basilica take Corso Mazzini, which is the main street leading off the square, lined with shops, and proceed to the Piazza Comune, the principal square of Assisi.

History

The Piazza Comune has an unbroken history since Roman times of being the hub of local government and commercial activity. If you look at Giotto's frescoes in the life cycle of St Francis in the Upper Basilica of St Francis you will see a picture of the Piazza Comune which is not that dissimilar to what we see now.

Tour

The outstanding feature of the square is the Church of Santa Maria sopra Minerva, which was so clearly once a Roman temple. Its present name suggests the dedication was to

Minerva but Castor and Pollux are also likely candidates. The pavement today lies at a higher level then during the Roman era and so you need to imagine twice the number of steps that you see today to get a good idea of how impressive the temple would have originally appeared. The temple was built in the first century BC and was linked to the forum by a street, which can still be seen in the Roman Museum nearby. Santa Maria started its life as a place of worship and still is today, but in the Middle Ages served for a time as a prison and magistrates' quarters. The interior is an anti-climax with its typical baroque decoration but provides a peaceful setting for a few moments' pause before returning to the square.

It was in the Piazza Comune that Francis spent time socializing with his many friends, by all accounts he enjoyed a good time and this zest for life he never lost. The Piazza also features in several episodes of his conversion to his new life of poverty and the forming of his community. Stand with the temple on your right and you are facing a nineteenth-century building at the end which is on the site of the medieval church of San Niccolo. Here Francis and his first few brothers opened the book of the Gospels three times (a common custom at the time) to discern their vocation, and found first the passage in Matthew where Christ's disciples are exhorted to sell everything they have and give it to the poor. On subsequent attempts they opened at: 'take nothing for your journey' (Luke 9:3) and 'if any man will follow me let him deny himself' (Matthew 16:21). The citizens of Assisi would also have witnessed Francis begging in the Piazza Comune for the money to repair churches and also ironically giving away the wealth of his first disciple the lawyer, Bernardo da Quintavalle. In spite of the attempts here to humiliate Francis the crowds flocked to honour him when he was canonized by Pope Gregory IX in the square in 1228, two years after his death.

The other buildings in the piazza date from shortly after Francis' lifetime but still occupy the site of previous houses and so the overall impression would have changed little. Next to the temple on the left is the Torre del Popolo (47 metres high) which was the first residence of the Captain of the People, an office similar to that of magistrate or chief of police (a later palace for the Captain was built on the left). At the top of the tower you see swallowtail crenellation which indicates a one-time affiliation to the Ghibelline faction (who supported the emperor), and at the base is a curious collection of different shaped blocks of stone set within a frame with an inscription above – this was a medieval form of checking that bricks, tiles, wood and cloth met the required standard in size and quality.

Opposite the temple you are faced by a complex of buildings which make up the Palazzi Comunali which were constructed at different periods to house the city government and the town hall is still housed here today as well as the Pinacoteca (art gallery). The earliest portion, to the left, is the Palazzo dei Priori which was completed in 1295 but the crenellation is a twentieth-century addition added in a 1920s restoration to make it look more authentic! During the Middle Ages the priors (government not ecclesiastic officials) would have occupied the top floor while downstairs grocers, tailors, barbers and butchers would have rented out space for their shops, a custom which continued until 1926.

Opening Times

Churches are generally open from 7.00am–12.00 and 3.00–7.00pm. It is best to avoid Sunday morning when mass is celebrated at various times and entry may not be permitted. The museum of San Rufino is open 10.00am–12.00 and 2.00–6.00pm (5.00pm in winter). Entrance fee payable

Facilities

There are public toilets (small charge) located very near the Chiesa Nuova or else in any of the many cafés en route.

Assisi: In the Footsteps of St Francis

There are a selection of cafés and souvenir shops in the Piazza Comune and Piazza Santa Chiara and in Corso Mazzini, the road which joins the two squares.

1. A view of Assisi

2. Near the Chiesa Nuova

3. The Chiesa Nuova, built over St Francis' family home

4. A tiny chapel marks the traditional site of St Francis' birthplace

5. San Rufino

6. Santa Maria sopra Minerva in Piazza Comune

7. The Upper Basilica of St Francis

8. Archway leading to Vicolo Sant' Andrea

9. The Lower Basilica of St Francis

10. Looking up to the Rocca Maggiore

Basilica of St Francis (San Francesco)

Upper Basilica of St Francis

Access

The basilica is situated at one end of the town, on two levels. The upper and the lower sections can be reached by a level path and road but inside the basilica it is only possible to go between the two by stairs. The tomb of St Francis is in the crypt below the lower basilica and can only be reached by stairs from here. The town bus stops nearby and the nearest car park (San Pietro) is below the basilica 5–10 minutes walk away.

If time permits, more than one visit to the basilica is advised as it is difficult to take in everything in one visit.

History

The Basilica of St Francis was built for one purpose – to house the remains of the great saint, whose popularity spread very rapidly across Europe and caused thousands of pilgrims to flock to Assisi. The idea for the basilica was in the mind of the pope at the time, Gregory IX, who as a cardinal had been the protector of the new Franciscan order and a great admirer of Francis, even before the canonization. A donation of land from a citizen of Assisi, of the hill just outside the city walls, allowed work to begin on the basilica as soon as Francis had been declared a saint, and money for the construction poured in from many sources with the promise from the pope of an indulgence for the donors. The land on which the basilica was built had been formerly used for executions and was popularly known as 'the Hill of Hell'. The name, of course, had to be altered and was soon rechristened as the 'Hill of Paradise'. The Lower Basilica was completed in record time – just two years, the upper church followed soon after and its consecration in 1253 marks a remarkable achievement. An alternative name for the Lower Basilica is the 'Cappella Papale' (Papal Chapel), as it was officially claimed by Pope Gregory IX as a papal residence.

LOWER BASILICA

Tour

Begin by walking down to the Lower Basilica. Don't be tempted to go into the top first and you will be rewarded for your patience.

Façade

It is hard to imagine the Lower Basilica as a building on its own but this was what was planned to start with and it was

designed to be a shrine, the resting place of the tomb of a saint, therefore, the interior is tomb-like, with little light let in and similar to a crypt in shape. Standing at the main door you are witnessing the act of faith of an ancient pilgrim, a Lady Berta who in her will left five poplar trees to be sold and the proceeds of which to pay for a new doorway. In a sense the whole basilica is a testimony to pilgrims of old, as without them and their financial support, it is unlikely that it could have ever been built. Before you go in just look down to the square which leads from the basilica with its elegant arcades on each side, these were created in the fifteenth century and offered shelter to the thousands who came to this shrine. All around this piazza would have been shops and souvenir stalls, where the pilgrim could have bought his hat badge and other memorabilia. It would have created a much livelier scene than what we see today!

As you enter into the basilica think of the medieval pilgrim. This would have been the last stage of his arduous pilgrimage and his goal was now in sight – the altar at the end of the nave where he could gain a glimpse of the tomb of the saint beneath it.

Nave

The area inside the door at the west end was a later addition to the original basilica which would not have appeared so

Basilica of St Francis (San Francesco)

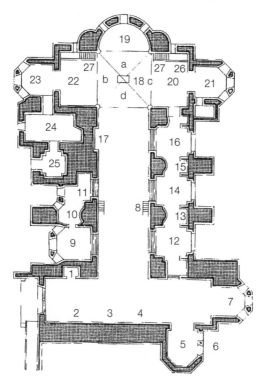

Lower Church

1 Cappella di San Sebastiano
2 Sepulchral monument of the
  Cerchi family
3 Choir
4 Sepulchral monument of John of
  Brienne
5 Cappella di Sant'Antonio Abate
6 Cemetery
7 Cappella di Santa Caterina
8 Entrance to the Crypt
9 Cappella di San Martino
10 Cappella Fontana
11 Cappella di Sant'Andrea
12 Cappella di Santo Stefano
13 Cappella di San Lorenzo
14 Cappella di Sant'Antonio Padua
15 Cappella di San Valentino
16 Cappella di Maria Maddalena

17 Platform of St Stanislas
18 Presbytery
19 Apse
20 Right transept
21 Cappella di San Nicola
22 Left transept
23 Cappella di San Giovanni Battista
24 Lower sacristy
25 Hidden sacristy
26 Chapter room
27 Stairs to the Cloister

a Glory of St Francis
b Allegory of Obedience
c Allegory of Chastity
d Allegory of Poverty

open and spacious as when it was completed in 1230. The shape of the basilica was not only to impress upon people its resemblance of a tomb, but also bring to mind that image peculiar to Francis and his followers of the Tau cross, the simple cross, which is borne out in the design of the church – the nave and cross transepts at the top of it forming a simple T-shape (see page 64 for more information of the Tau symbol).

Frescoes and decoration of the nave

The decoration of the Lower Basilica is of a simple nature, though the outstanding workmanship of it may now seem to contradict this. Fresco was the cheapest way of decorating walls and ceilings and in keeping with the Franciscan ideal of poverty, it was also useful as a method of instructing the pilgrims.

The decoration of the walls of the nave began soon after the completion of the basilica, around 1253 and the artist is not really known but simply identified the 'Master of St Francis' (Maestro di San Francesco). When originally built the basilica had no side chapels as it does now which break up the continuity of the walls, so that the sense of sequence and progression of the frescoes has been somewhat lost but imagine them as a series leading from one to the other, to be read together.

Frescoes on left wall

Facing the altar on the left-hand side are a series of frescoes representing the life of St Francis:

- St Francis renouncing all his wordly goods and ties by removing his clothes in front of the Bishop of Assisi and returning them to his father.
- The dream of Pope Innocent III in which he sees St Francis supporting the church.
- St Francis preaching to the birds.
- The stigmata of St Francis.
- The funeral of St Francis and recognition of the stigmata.

Frescoes on right wall

These frescoes depict scenes from the passion of Christ, which was so much a part of Francis' life and on which he meditated frequently:

- Christ is stripped of his garments and the preparation of the cross.
- The crucifixion.
- Taking down the body of Christ from the cross.
- Lamentation over the body of Christ.
- Christ appears on the road to Emmaus.

Chapels of interest

The side bays of the basilica have been opened up at various times since its construction to create chapels because of endowments by particular families, individuals or religious orders.

Chapel of St Martin (9)

This was built for a powerful Franciscan cardinal at the beginning of the fourteenth century and is particularly noted for the fresco life-cycle of St Martin by the great Sienese artist, Simone Martini. St Martin of Tours was often compared with St Francis because both had started out on their new lives in Christ by giving their possessions away to a poor man and this episode can be seen in the first panel on the bottom left-hand side.

Chapel of Mary Magdalen (16)

This was commissioned by the Franciscan Bishop of Assisi, Teobaldo Pontano da Todi, in 1296 and he can indeed be seen depicted in the frescoes as the Franciscan friar at the feet of Mary Magdalen. The majority of this work is thought to be by Giotto. Scenes on the left-hand wall show the supper in the house of Simon the Pharisee and the raising of Lazarus. On the right-hand side you can see 'Noli me tangere' ('Do not touch me') and the journey to Marseilles by Mary Magdalen.

There are many more chapels to see and their dedications are marked on the plan.

Altar area

Walk up the nave to the focal point of the basilica, the high altar beneath which is the tomb of St Francis. The opening in the altar was to allow the pilgrim to get as near as possible to the tomb of St Francis to venerate it as this was where the body was originally interred. The original frescoes painted by the Master of St Francis and Cimabue have been replaced by works by Lorenzetti and Giotto but a Maestà by Cimabue still remains.

Frescoes above the altar

These are concerned with an allegorical presentation of St Francis and represent the Franciscan virtues and the glory of St Francis.

(18a)	Glory of St Francis St Francis sits on a throne and is carried to heaven by angels.
(18b)	Allegory of Obedience Obedience is depicted by an old friar who places the yoke of obedience on another kneeling friar, assisted by prudence and humility.
(18c)	Allegory of Chastity Chastity is locked inside a castle tower, served by two angels. Outside the castle St Francis welcomes a friar, a Poor Clare and a layman, symbolizing the three Franciscan orders.
(18d)	Allegory of Poverty On top of a rock, Christ weds St Francis to poverty which is represented by a woman in ragged clothes.

Right transept (20)

Turn right from the altar into the right transept and look up into the vaulting. This is decorated with an astonishing series of eight scenes depicting the 'Childhood of Christ' and are considered to be some of the finest works by Giotto. The colours, variety in design and above all perspective were a great revolution and turning point in fourteenth-century art.

Standing with your back to the altar the scenes are on the right-hand side:

• top left – The Annunciation
• top right – The Visitation
• middle left – The Adoration of the Magi
• middle right – The Presentation in the Temple

On the left-hand side:

• top left – The Flight into Egypt
• top right – The Massacre of the Innocents
• middle left – Jesus debating in the Temple with the Teachers
• middle right – The Holy Family return to Nazareth

On the walls of this transept are scenes depicting miracles attributed to St Francis. On the right-hand side is a crucixion said to be by Giotto but also do not miss the Maestà by Cimabue at the bottom right-hand side of the vaulting. This dates from 1280 and must have been recognized in its day as a masterpiece because it was left when in the fourteenth century

all the other existing frescoes were covered over by those you see now. Note the stark portrait of St Francis which in its detail is very close to the descriptions of St Francis in the hagiographies written at the time of the case for Francis' canonization.

Left transept (22)

The vault of this transept is decorated with a cycle of frescoes painted by Pietro Lorenzetti in the 1320s, representing the passion of Christ. Standing with your back to the altar the scenes are on the right-hand side:

• top left – The Entry into Jerusalem
• top right – The Last Supper
• middle left – The Washing of the Feet
• middle right – Christ's Arrest in the Garden of Olives
• bottom left – The Suicide of Judas
• bottom of right – St Francis receiving the stigmata on La Verna

On the left-hand side:

• top left – The Scourging of Christ at the Pillar
• top right – The Carrying of the Cross
• bottom – The Crucifixion (The damage to this fresco was a result of an altar being placed in front of it in 1604 and removed in 1870!)

Above the archway into the Chapel of St John the Baptist are scenes depicting:

- bottom left – Taking down of Christ from the Cross
- bottom right – Placing Christ in the Tomb
- top left – Christ descends into Limbo
- top right – The Resurrection

Note the fresco beneath the crucifixion scene on the left, also by Lorenzetti. This depicts Our Lady with the Christ Child with St John the Evangelist and St Francis on either side of her. However, it is popularly called, 'The Madonna of the Sunsets' (la Madonna dei Tramonti) because when the light from the sunset filters through the door it illuminates this picture, giving a very ethereal quality. An interpretation of this fresco is that the baby Jesus is asking his mother who loves him most and Our Lady replies that St Francis does, by indicating her answer with her thumb.

Relics of St Francis in the chapter house (26)

The original chapter house of the monastery is now used to house a unique collection of the relics of St Francis, which should not be missed if this room is open. Among the things on show in the cases are:

- A chalice and patten used by St Francis, two linen cloths used by Jacopa di Settesoli to wipe St Francis' forehead when on his deathbed.
- A hair shirt worn by St Francis.
- A horn given to Francis as a gift by the Sultan of Egypt.

- The Bull of Solet Annuere, the confirmation of the Rule of St Francis, sent to him by Pope Honorius III in 1223.
- The stone on which St Francis' head rested in the tomb, coins and other objects found in the tomb when it was opened in 1818.
- Items of clothing belonging to the saint including a tunic and the felt boots made by St Clare for him to protect his feet from the effects of the stigmata. A piece of felt which St Francis used to cover the stigmata wound in his side.
- A sheet of parchment on which St Francis wrote a version of the Divine Praises and which he sent to Brother Leo. (Note the Tau symbol used.)

TOMB OF ST FRANCIS (8)

The entrance to this is halfway up the nave on your right and down a flight of stairs.

The crypt was not part of the original church, it was excavated in 1818 in order to verify that the tomb of St Francis was really below the high altar. The body of Francis had been placed down here in order to protect it from being stolen, as the trade in relics was a particularly lucrative one and it would have been seen as a great asset for a neighbouring and rival city like Perugia.

Before you go through the wrought iron screen into the crypt, note the little plaque on the wall behind you which has the name 'Jacopa di Settesoli' on it. Jacopa was a wealthy widow and a great admirer and friend of St Francis. She wanted to attend Francis on his deathbed but his brothers protested that she could not as she was a woman. However, St Francis solved the problem by making her an honorary Franciscan brother! She was buried in this place in recognition of her devotion.

The tomb of St Francis is enclosed by iron grating behind the altar in a solid block of stone. The oil for the votive lamp is provided by various Italian cities in turn.

If you go behind the tomb and look on the wall you will see the tombs of four of St Francis' first companions: Rufino, Angelo, Masseo and Leo, which were placed here in 1932.

After visiting the Lower Basilica you can go up to the Upper Basilica either by going back through the entrance you came in by and walking up the road, or using the internal staircase that connects the two, which can be reached by the door behind the main altar. If you use the stairs on your way up you will come out of the church and overlook the cloister built by the Franciscan Pope Sixtus IV in 1476. In fact the cloister forms part of the papal palace and the Lower Basilica is also known by the name of Cappella Papale (Papal Chapel) and illustrates the allegiance

that the Franciscan order has always had to the papacy.

UPPER BASILICA
When you enter the Upper Basilica from the Lower Basilica you come in by the main altar and the best way to visit the church is to view the presbytery area and transepts before following the life-cycle frescoes around the church. The plan of the Upper Basilica is a classical Franciscan one of a plain wide open nave with a single crossing near the altar to facilitate preaching and thanks to what must have been a very fast flow of donations – the building was finished in twenty years. According to normal Franciscan dictates the decoration of the basilica should have been plainer and the use of glass confined to four panels behind the main altar, however, Assisi was an Apostolic See and although the design is not over elaborate there is more adornment than usual for a Franciscan church.

Stand still and look around you; into the transepts, behind in the apse, in front along the nave to the west door and above you to the windows and ceilings, don't you feel a strong sense of harmony in what you see? The great success of the Upper Basilica is a sense of unity of purpose in its design, in spite of the number of people who were involved in the building of it and the decoration, because the motivation was very clear – to create a great monument in honour of a saint who had had such an influence on so many in all walks of society.

Apse and transepts

Stand facing the high altar and notice the magnificent stained glass windows, which date from 1235 to 1250 and were the first of their kind in Italy and help so effectively to illuminate the church. It is difficult to make out any of the detail from this distance but a detailed guide book will show you what you are missing. At the back of the apse is the papal throne raised up on a dais, in front of which stands the main altar made of the local pinkish stone, which was consecrated by Innocent IV in 1253.

On both sides of the apse are ranged 102 choir stalls made at the end of the fifteenth century. They deserve particular attention on account of the wonderful perspective achieved in the marquetry inlay panels featuring scenes of still life, books and musical instruments.

Look behind the choir stalls and the papal throne and you will be rewarded with a series of frescoes painted by the great Florentine master, Cimabue, in the late thirteenth century. They depict scenes from the life of the Virgin Mary and are from left to right; Mary leaving the apostles; the death of Mary; the Assumption of Mary; and Christ and Mary enthroned.

Cimabue's work continues in the left transept but unfortunately the white lead pigment has oxidized over the years turning it black and resulting in an effect not dissimilar to a photographic negative. The Crucifixion is, however, a masterpiece of its time and in spite of its condition the terrible sadness of this event is impressed on the viewer and conveyed particularly through Our Lady with her arms outstretched and St Francis weeping at the foot of the cross. Cimabue's workshops were largely responsible for the frescoes in the right-hand transept which are mainly concerned with the mission and death of St Peter.

The frescoes in the nave

Looking up the nave towards the main door you cannot help but be struck by the cycle of frescoes around the lower part of the walls featuring events from the life of St Francis. Look again though and you will see that there are in fact two series of tableaux at work; an upper and lower one.

With your back to the main altar you need to start on the left-hand side of the church. The upper register is concerned with the Old Testament and on the lower half begins the story of Francis for all to see and easily comprehend. The juxtaposition of the life of Francis and the Old and New Testament episodes has a clear message, that Francis' evangelical mission follows on from the work of the prophets, Jesus and his apostles.

Did Giotto paint the frescoes?

The authorship of the St Francis frescoes is now keenly debated. For many years the artist was thought to be Giotto but there are now doubts because on close inspection the brush work does not seem to match that of his other works, and recent investigation by experts has linked these paintings to the Roman artist, Pietro Cavallini. No matter who the painter was the fact remains that these scenes are most remarkable for not only being of the highest order artistically but also for the way in which they show us the enormous effect that Francis had on this period for such a work to have been commissioned.

The 28 panels concerning St Francis start with the incident that was felt to be the beginning of his great mission rather than his birth and the themes are as follows (starting on the left wall as you stand with your back to the high altar in the transept):

1. An ordinary man honours St Francis

The scene is set in the Piazza Commune in Assisi with the Roman church and the Palace of the Captain of the People clearly visible and recalls an event which happened before Francis abandoned his wordly life indicated by the rich clothes he wears. The citizen of Assisi recognizes Francis' future greatness before the saint had even recognized his vocation.

2. Francis gives his cloak to a poor knight

This is probably the first scene that was painted and shows Francis still dressed as the son of a wealthy man, meeting a knight who has fallen on hard times and responding with unconditional charity by offering his own cloak. The event takes place outside Assisi, as you can see in the top left of the painting on the right the Abbey of San Benedetto, who rented the Porziuncula (the 'little portion' of land at Santa Maria degli Angeli) to Francis.

3. Dream of the palace

When unsure of his future after he had returned from prison in Perugia Francis had an idea that he ought to go south and join the forces of Walter de Brienne fighting the emperor. He reached Spoleto where he was forced to his bed because of illness and during this time he had a dream which featured a palace full of coats of arms and banners emblazoned with the cross of Christ. Francis asks Christ who they are for and receives the answer that they are intended for him and all his knights. Christ challenges Francis further, demanding why he seeks to serve a servant rather than God, the master.

Francis then enquires as to what he should do and he is told emphatically to return home where he will learn what it is he has to do.

4. *The miracle of the crucifix*

This tableau describes the day Francis went to the dilapidated Church of San Damiano where he received further instruction from Christ while he was praying before the crucifix, 'Go, Francis and repair my house which is falling into ruin.'

5. *Francis renounces his worldly possessions*

The conflict between Francis and his father, Pietro di Bernadone is finally resolved in this most dramatic meeting in front of Bishop Guido of Assisi, who was one of Francis' greatest supporters. Francis gives back all he has that belongs to Pietro, thus releasing him from any legal obligation to his father. He makes the separation very clear by announcing that he now only has one father, his father in heaven. In the top left-hand side you can see a hand blessing St Francis. (At one time there may have been more of the heavenly body visible but there has been some deterioration, so it is hard to tell.)

6. *Dream of Innocent III*

This is the first time that Francis is depicted in a habit and here he is fulfilling the message of San Damiano. Pope Innocent III sees him in a dream holding up the church which is in danger of toppling over (representing the threat to the Church from heretical groups and temporal powers). This image confirms that Francis was to actively promote orthodoxy in his teachings and a profound respect for the authority of the Holy Father and the priests that was handed down from Christ via his apostles.

7. *The confirmation of the Rule*

Francis went to Rome in 1209 to gain an authorization from the pope for the way of life for himself and his brothers in order that they would be officially allowed to preach. Innocent confirms the approval of the church by letting them be tonsured (as they are portrayed in this scene). The verbal approval has been seen by some as a noncommittal one on the part of the pope, but it should be taken into account that the practice of a written Rule was not formally introduced until the reforms of the fourth Lateran Council a few years later. It is also worth looking up to the fresco in the upper section in which you can see Isaac blessing Jacob. The message here is that both Francis and Jacob are founding fathers of two stages in the history of God's people.

8. *Vision of the flaming chariot*

Some of the brothers are in the hovel at Rivotorto and they see Francis (who was in Assisi at the time) carried away in a chariot like Elijah. This comparison with the great prophet was a sign to the companions that Francis would lead them just like Elijah led the Israelites.

9. *Vision of the thrones*

In this panel Leo, whom Francis called 'the little lamb of God' is shown a vision of heaven in a dream. An angel indicates that there is a throne reserved for Francis in paradise, which is raised higher than any other. It was the one once occupied by the devil himself and as the proud are fallen so must humble Francis be exalted.

10. *Exorcizing the demons from Arezzo*

Francis is the kneeling figure on the left and in front of him is Brother Silvester (formerly a canon at the cathedral of San Rufino in Assisi) who has been sent on in advance to the city of Arezzo in Tuscany to expel the demons. Demons represent avarice, greed, excessive power and political ambition, which many preachers railed against during the medieval period.

11. *Trial by fire*

Francis felt an enormous need to go to the Holy Land to preach peace to those undertaking the crusade. In spite of the danger Francis and Brother Illuminato ventured into the Saracen camp and challenged the Sultan's priests to an ordeal by fire but they would not join in! Although Francis did not succeed in converting the Sultan, he obviously gained his respect as he was allowed to leave and furthermore was given gifts, which are now on display in the chapel of reliquaries in the Lower Basilica.

12. *St Francis in ecstacy*

The heart of Francis' life was prayer and devotion and in this scene we see him being elevated at the height of his ecstacy while in contemplation and receiving the blessing of Christ.

13. *The crib at Greccio*

This painting recalls the events of Christmas Eve, 1223 when Francis wanted to celebrate Christmas and the divine incarnation in a real way for the benefit of all the citizens of Greccio. Francis (in his deacon's robes) is shown as he was reportedly seen by John of Velita at the crib holding the Christ child (although the bed was empty). The artist has taken some licence with this event by showing it taking place in a church, whereas it was in the open and by placing the women in their proper place behind the screen at the back!

14. *The miracle of the spring* (left of the main door)

Towards the end of his life in 1224 Francis goes to Mount La Verna to spend time in contemplation at the sanctuary there and on his way he is offered the use of a donkey by a man who then follows him. The poor man becomes very thirsty and ill as they approach the mountain and begs Francis to find him a drink, whereupon Francis strikes the rock in the tradition of Moses and a spring appears.

15. *Francis preaches to the birds* (right of the main door)

This is perhaps the most famous image of Francis giving a sermon to the birds at a place called Pian d'Arca not far from Assisi, and telling them to remember to praise their creator who had given them their wings and feathers as clothes and the sky for their home. Francis' inclusion of nature in his ministry was not a sentimental affection but a deep love for anything that was part of God's creation because it contained God.

16. *Death of the knight of Celano*

During a journey in the Abruzzo region, Francis is welcomed into the home of a knight in the town of Celano (perhaps he was even a relative of Francis' first biographer and Franciscan brother, Thomas of Celano). The knight is told of his imminent death and thus has time to confess his sins and prepare himself, a reward for welcoming Francis into his house.

17. *Francis preaches before Pope Honorius III*

Francis appears before Pope Honorius III to ask him to formally ratify the Rule of the order which had been approved of orally in 1209 by the previous pope. At the time for him to speak Francis is dumbstruck but he asks for help from the Holy Spirit and the concentrated expressions of the pope and his curia attest to the success of divine intervention.

18. *Francis appears to his brothers in Arles*

St Anthony of Padua featured on the left (looking rather bloated on account of suffering from dropsy) has convened a chapter meeting in Arles in France and during a discussion on the meaning of the inscription on the cross 'INRI', Francis appears miraculously before them bestowing his blessing on them.

19. *Francis receives the stigmata at La Verna*

Francis sought all his life to be totally identified with Christ and he continually prayed for this end. This event which occurred just two years before his death was what St Bonaventure called 'the alpha and omega', the completion of Francis' life's mission and yet the beginning of his future of union with Christ. Francis was at the sanctuary of La Verna and during the night of the feast of the Exultation of the Cross he had a vision of a seraph and afterwards found that he bore the imprints of the wounds of Christ's passion. This was the first recorded instance of the stigmata being received and was the perfect proof of the humanity and suffering of Jesus.

20. *Death of St Francis*

Francis, aware that he was near death, insisted that he return to the Porziuncula, which he loved so well and it was here on the evening of 3 October 1226 that he died, after blessing each of his brothers. In this scene there is much sorrow at the death of their spiritual father but at the same time we see Francis being borne by the angels to heaven, for one brother attested that he had seen Francis' soul rise heavenwards in the guise of a star.

21. *Apparition of Francis to Brother Agostino and Bishop Guido*

This scene shows two concurrent events; on the left is Brother Agostino on his deathbed in a Franciscan community in the Campania region. He had been dumb for some time but he was heard to cry out to Francis to tell him to wait and he would go with him, shortly after which he died. On the right we see Bishop Guido of Assisi, Francis' long-time friend and supporter who was on a pilgrimage to the shrine of St Michael in Gargagno at the time of Francis' death but knew in a dream that Francis had died and was going to heaven.

22. *Verification of the stigmata*

Here we see Francis being taken in procession from the Porziuncula up into Assisi. A learned man of the city called, Girolamo stops the cortège to verify Francis' stigmata in an episode that is redolant of the apostle Thomas after Christ has risen from the dead.

23. *The Poor Clares mourn Francis*

Artistic licence intervenes once again by allowing Clare and her sisters to step outside their convent building to see Francis for the last time. In reality they would have only been able to view the funeral litter from the small grate through which they were normally given communion. The artist has created a scene filled with emotion and yet another comparison with the Gospels by featuring a person climbing a tree for a better view, rather like Zacchaeus.

24. The canonization of St Francis

Just under two years after Francis' death Pope Gregory IX decided that there had been enough evidence gathered to declare that Francis was truly a saint in heaven and the ceremony took place in the Piazza Comune in Assisi. The day after the canonization the pope laid the foundation stone of the Basilica of St Francis on the Colle del Paradiso (Hill of Paradise).

25. Dream of Gregory IX

The last four frescoes are all concerned with miracles of St Francis. In this first one we see Pope Gregory IX who although he had promoted the canonization of Francis still had doubts (like Thomas) about the veracity of Francis' stigmata. In a dream Francis shows Gregory his wounds and asks the pope to fetch a phial in which to catch the blood that flows from the injury. Gregory obeys this command and the container seems to fill up to the brim with blood and from that time on the pope harbours no more doubts.

26. The man of Lerida is healed

This panel demonstrates Francis' great healing power performed on a man not in Italy but far away in Spain. Giovanni di Castro is at death's door as a result of having been ambushed and prays to Francis in his anguish. The saint appears and cures Giovanni by laying his wounded hands on him because of the faith he has shown.

27. The confession of the woman of Benevento

This miracle like the others portrayed in these four last panels does not occur in Assisi, thus testifying to Francis' tremendous powers of intervention now that he resides in heaven. A woman from Benevento appears to die and the mourners begin the wake when she wakes up and calls for a priest to hear her confession. In her lifetime she had been devoted to St Francis and she says that it was he who had intervened to allow her to return to her body to confess a serious sin that she had never revealed. She makes a sincere confession then dies in peace, a devil leaves disappointed followed in hot pursuit by an angel.

28. The freeing of Pietro the heretic

Pietro was accused of heresy while in Rome and was thrown

into a dark dungeon with almost nothing to eat. The experience deeply affected him and on the eve of the feast of St Francis he appeals to the saint for help, promising that he has reformed and now recants his heresy. Francis takes pity on him, enters the cell and breaks his chains but Pietro is too stunned to escape and instead summons the guards with his shouting, who in turn call for the bishop. The bishop realizing what has happened falls on his knees and gave thanks to God.

Opening Times

Both the Upper and Lower Basilicas are generally open from about 6.30am until sunset (although in January and February may be shut at lunchtime). However, to see the east end of the lower church illuminated inside it is best to avoid 12.30–2.00pm and after 5.00pm. On Sundays and religious feast days it is not advisable to visit the lower basilica when masses are being celebrated. Mass is celebrated early morning and evening in the crypt – please consult the noticeboards in the basilica for further details.

Facilities

Public toilets can be found opposite the green in front of the Upper Basilica. There are cafés in the Via San Francesco and below the basilica towards San Pietro. For a good range of religious souvenirs visit the repository which can be accessed when you go from the Lower to the Upper Basilica by the stairs.

Quiet Corners of Assisi

Spending a day in Assisi it is easy to think that you have seen everything there is to see but, those who stay find even a week not enough to discover all Assisi's nooks and crannies. Below are some suggestions for other directions to take once you have seen the great sights of the city, but there is no doubt that by simply meandering you will find your own favourite corner.

Rocca Maggiore – Piazza Vescovado and Santa Maria Maggiore – Santo Stefano and Porta San Giacomo – Roman Assisi

ROCCA MAGGIORE

You cannot miss the fortress of Rocca Maggiore, it lords it over the city of Assisi below, as indeed was its purpose. This vast defensive building dominates the skyline from every angle as at many times in the past it dominated the lives of the people, and Francis himself is thought to have been part of the attacking force of 1198 that demolished a previous version. A visit to the Rocca Maggiore makes a relaxing and fascinating break, it takes you out of the town, offers fantastic panoramic views of the surrounding countryside and another glimpse of Assisi's past.

Access

The Rocca Maggiore fortress can be reached on foot by taking the steps that lead up from Via San Rufino (on the left as you are walking up to the cathedral) past the San Rufino Hotel, at the top you meet the road and turn left, the castle is in front of you. The walk is not particularly arduous but not recommended for anyone with walking difficulties. Alternatively it is a short taxi ride.

History

A fortification has existed here from at least the sixth century and because of its ideal position it was adopted as the stronghold of the Duke of Spoleto, Conrad of Urslingen, under the sovereignty of the emperor in 1174. Constant conflict between the papacy and the emperor led to Conrad abandoning it in 1198 allowing the people of Assisi (homines populi) to tear it down and the municipality gained the promise from the emperor at the beginning of the thirteenth century that the fortress would not be rebuilt. For over 150 years the townspeople had their way but with the return of the pope from Avignon a reassertion of papal authority arrived in the person of

Cardinal Albornoz who seized much of Umbria for the papacy and thanks to him the fortress rose again to be a symbol of peace and stability. This more tranquil state of affairs did not last long and over the next two hundred years various nobles and soldiers of fortune took control of the Rocca and imprisoned their opponents inside. With the return of papal rule in the sixteenth century the castle fell into obscurity and decline and did not see happier days until the 1880s when the town council of Assisi bought it and restored it as a tourist attraction.

Tour

The curtain walls

The present-day entrance into the castle is the original one and impresses upon you the defensive purpose of this building. Although the outer walls are now partially in ruin it is not difficult to imagine how hard it would have been to scale them. At first glance it may seem they are solid but in fact they had to be accessible in order to be an effective means of protecting the stronghold, so an interior passage runs all the way around and connects the towers which were used as look-out posts as well as being vantage points for attacking any assailants.

It is still possible to go along inside part of the walls but as there are no lights you will

need to bring a torch with you or hire one at the ticket office. At the end of the north-west wall you can climb up the polygonal tower, now equipped with a staircase but in the Middle Ages there was only a retractable ladder for security.

The stronghold and keep

Inside the great walls you come to the heart of the castle where if all else failed the inhabitants would lock themselves in and prepare to resist the besieging forces. The entry gate was originally protected by a portcullis and leads into the courtyard around which were the living quarters for the governing family, servants and troops. You can still go into some of these rooms although others have long since been destroyed or crumbled into decay. The tower-like corner of the stronghold is the keep which would have been taller than it is now and also completely cut off from the rest of the castle to provide further security in the event of the fortress being stormed. You can now pass into the keep by means of a wooden footbridge but this was in fact a drawbridge attached to the wall by a chain mechanism which could be lowered or raised as required. It is possible to climb up to the fourth floor, although this is now without a roof. It is worth noting that the chambers on the second floor were used as a prison until 1600.

PIAZZA VESCOVADO AND SANTA MARIA MAGGIORE

Access

You can reach Piazza Vescovado either by taking the road down from the Piazza Comune and past the Chiesa Nuova or descending from Piazza Santa Chiara by way of Via Sant'Agnese. In both cases it is only a short walk.

History

It is probable that the site now occupied by Santa Maria Maggiore was the location of the first cathedral of Assisi founded by St Savino, the second Bishop of Assisi in the fourth century and excavations have confirmed the existence of a Roman dwelling here and the finds have included an eighth–century sarcophagus. The church went through various enlargements and renovations but the title of cathedral was transferred to San Rufino in the eleventh century. However Maria Maggiore still kept its episcopal seat and the bishop's palace (Palazzo del Vescovado) remained, as it still does today, to the side of the church.

For St Francis this small square was to witness one of the pivotal events of his life when he categorically confirmed his intention to follow poverty. Pietro di Bernadone, Francis' father, had hoped that his son would come to his senses after his time in Perugia as a prisoner of war, but his patience must have been sorely tried when Francis sold cloth in order to finance the restoration of San Damiano. We can only guess at how Pietro must have felt towards his son at this time but probably like many fathers he felt that a short, sharp shock might jolt him out of his odd behaviour and back on to what he saw as the straight and narrow. What is documented is that Pietro approached Bishop Guido to adjudicate in the matter of the missing cloth and all three parties met in front of the bishop's lodgings in this square. Pietro must have first felt vindicated when Guido instructed Francis to return his father's property to him, but the satisfaction was short-lived as Francis quite literally gave his father everything he had received from him right down to his under-clothes! It is said that Guido quickly wrapped Francis in a servant's cloak but the saint was not to be stopped and he calmly announced that Pietro was no longer his father as that title could be accorded only to his father in heaven. What became of Francis' family after this event is not known unfortunately and certainly there is no record of any reconciliation, although it is hard to imagine Mona Pica not having been present in her son's life in some way from this point on.

Tour

The square provides a place for calm respite especially in the heat and is a pleasant place to sit for a few moments while taking in the grand houses which surround it and once were the residences of the rich. It is quite safe to drink the water from the sixteenth-century fountain (as it is from any in Assisi) which is curiously called the Lion Fountain, for originally there was one and the water spouted from the mouth, but this was later replaced by the pine cone you see today.

Santa Maria Maggiore is tucked into the corner and easy to miss but well worth the visit. The interior may be simple but it is perhaps one of the most charming in Assisi as it has not been the victim of baroque additions or adaptations. Unfortunately, the earthquake of 1832 caused much of the wall frescoes to be lost, but you can still see some fragments featuring images of Mary, as this church is dedicated to her.

SANTO STEFANO AND PORTA SAN GIACOMO

Access

From the Piazza Comune take the upper road (Via San Paolo) on the right towards the Basilica of St Francis and Santo Stefano is reached by the stairs on the left. To reach Porta San Giacomo you just continue along the same street.

History

Santo Stefano is situated in a quiet and picturesque corner of Assisi and has been part of the scenery for more than eight hundred years and would

certainly have been known to Francis and Clare. It is this simple church which is said to have been awarded the particular honour of bearing the tidings of Francis' death before it was publicly known, as its bells tolled spontaneously at that moment. Along the Via San Paolo follow a route which would have been in the process of being built during Francis' time, ending in the gate, Porta San Giacomo, constructed as part of the new fourteenth-century walls but which followed the Roman pattern.

Tour

Santo Stefano has one of the most beautiful settings of any church in Assisi and one which is easily able to impress upon the visitor an atmosphere of peace and tranquillity. Very simply built from the pink Monte Subasio stone you feel sure Francis himself would have approved of the design and it is a place that many feel able to just sit in and reflect quietly. There are some remains of frescoes on the walls but little else by way of decoration or embellishment.

As was often the case in the Middle Ages the church was the centre of social life and the main source of any charitable work, and this church was no exception organizing a Confraternity of St Stephen, which ran a hospital in a building nearby. Each year on St Stephen's Day, 26 December, the Confraternity process here dressed in their robes to celebrate masses for the feast of their patron.

Continue along the Via San Paolo which, although it may seem rather quiet after the main square, shows another aspect of the expansion that took place in medieval Assisi, as the city grew more prosperous and populated. On the left-hand side of the road you will pass a rather unassuming building which a careful examination of the small plaque by the door tells you is called CEFID (which translated from the Italian stands for the Ecumenical Centre for Dialogue between all Faiths). Here people of all religions who are interested in and inspired by St Francis are welcomed by the Franciscan order as the message of Francis transcends the barriers of race and creed and it is no surprise that Pope John Paul II has chosen Assisi as the place to which he invites leaders of other faiths for discussions.

Via San Paolo becomes Via Metastasio and descending towards the Porta San Giacomo you come to almost a ninety degree bend in the road where you will see on your left one of the loveliest corners of Assisi approached through the low arch of Sant'Andrea. The winding Vicolo Sant'Andrea will take you through a typical medieval quarter to its parish church, Santa Margherita, dating from the thirteenth century and even possessing its own tiny square in front. Assisi

may not seem that large to us today but centuries ago it was divided into many different sections, each with their own character and infrastructure.

Via Metastasio turns into Via San Giacomo which before it wends its way down to the Basilica of St Francis reaches one of the ancient gates of the city, Porta San Giacomo (Saint James). Although the gate has no battlements or sheltered area on top this has not stopped a cypress tree planting itself and surviving there for at least one hundred and fifty years.

ROMAN ASSISI

Even the German poet Goethe was very impressed by the Roman temple, now the Church of Santa Maria sopra Minerva in the Piazza Comune, but it is easy to see this in isolation and miss many of the other remains of Assisi's ancient heritage. Just a few steps from the Piazza Comune is the Archaeological Museum in Via Portica also called the Foro Romano but this is probably inaccurate as it is now thought that the forum was located in Piazza San Rufino. It is more likely that the Piazza Comune was the religious centre of Assisi and in the museum you can walk along the original street that reached the temple as well as see many of the finds that have been excavated.

There is no doubt that Assisi was a Roman town of some importance and would have possessed all those buildings that attested to its status even if few of them are still visible. Leaving the main square and going uphill to San Rufino you pass over the areas that would have formed the forum and theatre and reach what would have been the upper terraces of the town in Piazza Matteotti which was a necropolis and in the corner of which near the cathedral you can see the remains of tombs dating from the first century AD. Climb further still and you will come across the remains of the Amphitheatre in the Via del Anfiteatro Romano, the shape of which gives away the original purpose of this site, go into the courtyard of the Hotel Anfiteatro for a better view.

Practical Information

Rocca Maggiore Open 9.00am-dusk (not closed for lunch) entrance fee payable. There are toilets here and a small café.

Santa Maria Maggiore Open from early morning to evening but closed 12.00–3.00pm

Santo Stefano Open from early morning to evening but closed 12.00–3.00pm (approximately)

Archaeological Museum Open daily mid-October to mid-March 10.00am–1.00pm and 2–5.00pm; mid-March to mid-October 10.00am–1.00pm and 3–7.00pm. Entrance fee payable

---

Assisi Festivals

Calendimaggio Takes place every year on the first weekend following the 1st of May and celebrates the arrival of spring. The historical upper and lower sections of the town dress in medieval costume and compete against each other in a number of events

Feast of St Clare Celebrated on 11 August with processions and high mass

Feast of St Francis Celebrated on 3 and 4 October each year with civil processions and special religious services and festivities

---

The Hermitage (Carceri)

Many people visiting Assisi do not make it up to the Hermitage and some never know of its existence, which is a great shame as those who have made it comment on its great atmosphere and spirit which helps us to begin to understand the essence of Francis' ideals. Assisi tells of Francis' early life and the public acclamation after his death, but at the Hermitage we learn of the importance to him of profound meditation and prayer, which were the necessary foundation to his evangelical work in the world.

View of the Hermitage

Access

The road up to the Hermitage is steep, narrow and winding and therefore, not suitable for coaches or buses which means no public transport is available. For the hardy it is quite possible to walk up to the Hermitage either by road from Piazza Matteotti and through the Porta dei Cappuccini, or footpath via Rocca Minore (about 4 kilometres). In spring or autumn this can make a very pleasant excursion, with the opportunity for a picnic (there is an area with benches near to the Hermitage in the woods). Alternatively, you can take a taxi from the rank near St Clare's Basilica and the taxi driver will normally wait for you at the Hermitage for about forty-five minutes. A visit to the Hermitage by taxi can quite easily be combined with seeing San Damiano, just ask the driver when you start out.

History and background

Francis' choice for a place of retreat and meditation was often governed by tradition and in this the Hermitage is no exception, as there had probably been a shelter for hermits here since early Christian times. The crude chapel at the heart of this anchorage was dedicated to Santa Maria Carcerum, Our Lady of the Prisons, referring to the solitary nature of the place and the setting oneself apart from the world in order to draw closer to God. We do not know how often Francis came

to this place but that he did is without doubt, and that he thought withdrawing to such places was vital for himself and his brothers we can also be sure of. The Hermitage of Assisi is but one of many that Francis founded and considering that Francis did not want the religious life of his community based around a building, as was the case with most other orders of the time, we can appreciate the importance that he attached to the need for prayerful retreat.

The Hermitage as we see it today hides the rudimentary caves that made up the retreat centre of Francis' time and so it is necessary to apply one's imagination and try and ignore the neat and attractive buildings added by St Bonaventure and then St Bernardine in order to gain a clearer vision of the original purpose of this place.

Tour

Whether you arrive on foot or by car, your visit starts by entering the gates to the Hermitage and the rather unwelcoming sign that warns you of the possible presence of adders in the woods! A wooden notice shows the area of the Hermitage mapped out and all the paths it is possible to follow and the situation of the various grottoes that have been found in the woods. Carry on (about 300 metres) along the path surrounded by ilex trees until you descend a little to enter the monastery complex and you find yourself in a picturesque courtyard. It is worth pausing here awhile, notice on the wall of the building, the symbol of the rising sun enclosing the letters IHS (which stand for Iesus Huius et Salvator – Jesus, Son and Saviour), which was the insignia of St Bernardine of Siena, the great Franciscan preacher of the fifteenth century. Take in the view from the outer wall, for a fine sight of the wooded hillside and the monastery.

While resting here it is appropriate to consider what St Francis himself said of how those withdrawing to the Hermitage should both occupy and organize themselves:

Those who wish to live religiously in hermitages should be three brothers or four at the most; two of these should be mothers and they should have two sons or at least one. The two who are mothers should follow the life of Martha while the two sons should follow the life of Mary and they may have an enclosure in which each one may have his small cell in which he may pray and sleep.

And in the enclosure, they should not permit any person to enter, nor should they eat there. Those brothers who are the mothers should be eager to stay far from every person; and because of the obedience to their minister they should protect their sons from everyone, so that no one can talk with them. And any sons should not talk with any person except with

their mothers and the minister. The sons should, however, assume the role of mothers, as from time to time it may be good for them to exchange roles.

Francis' grotto

Enter the buildings opposite the archway you have just come through, behind the well and you find yourself taken back to the primitive rooms that Francis and his brothers helped to create, first of all a small chapel called the Cappella di San Bernardino, which then leads into the chapel of Santa Maria delle Carceri. Be vigilant going down the steep and narrow staircase (there is a one-way system in operation, so you shouldn't meet someone coming the other way, but that's not to say it hasn't been tried!). Don't rush through the small chamber, carved out of the bedrock, that you now meet, as this was St Francis' room – a fact recognized by the floral tribute that is always left there; some people leave coins here but for no apparent good reason. Behind the balustrade is the original rockface or Francis' bed, calling it this is not just fanciful as there are several references in the lives written about him that he only accepted sleep with the greatest reluctance and saw it as a lost opportunity for time at prayer. Hence, Francis attempted to prevent himself from falling asleep by creating the most uncomfortable bed for himself that he could.

From the grotto you exit through the tiny chapel and if you can take your time here it is well worth while because it conveys as well as anywhere that original spirit of Francis – of all humility, of having nothing more than the absolutely essential. Coming out of this chapel look back on the wall and you will see an early, if very faded, fresco of St Francis preaching to the birds. One tradition has this event happening here at the Hermitage and in this setting it is easy to imagine it.

The grounds of the Hermitage

A small path takes you up from the grotto to around the back of the monastery and a view across the valley below. On the slope just near the path is an ilex tree which is heavily strapped and supported because this tree is said to have been here at the time of Francis and on which the birds perched while Francis preached to them. Tradition aside, birds, trees and caves which are now romantically named after Francis and his followers, all help to impress on us the importance of nature to Francis. Francis saw in all God's creation God himself and his attachment to the natural world was not some mere sentimental notion but a real love of the creator, and it is easier to understand this up at the Hermitage on Monte Subasio than anywhere.

Continuing round the path you

meet two sculptures, the first is *Francis Freeing the Doves* (dating from the late nineteenth century) and the second a much more recent work (1998) is called the *Ecstacy of St Francis*, with the saint lying prostrate and his brothers sitting on the ground marking out the constellations of the night sky with a divining rod. The whole of this woodland walk (the Viale di San Francesco) is very conducive to meditation and it is easy to see why those seeking a place for contemplation and reflection have come here over the centuries and the reason for this area continuing to be a haven of peace. The outside altar serves as an opportune spot for stopping and reading St Francis' great poem lauding God's creation, 'The Canticle of the Creatures' written at San Damiano.

The Canticle of the Creatures
(*composed 1224/1225*)

> *Most high, all-powerful, good Lord,*
> *all praise be yours, all glory, all honour*
> *and all blessing.*
> *To you alone, Most High, do they belong.*
> *No mortal lips are worthy to pronounce your name.*
>
> *All praise be yours, my Lord,*
> *in all your creatures,*
> *especially Sir Brother Sun who brings the day;*
> *and light you give us through him.*

Statue of St Francis and a Young Boy

How beautiful he is, how radiant in his splendour!
Of you, Most High, he is the token.

All praise be yours, my Lord for Sister Moon and the Stars; in the heavens you have made them, bright and precious and fair.

All praise be yours, my Lord, for Sister Water; she is so useful and lowly, so precious and pure.

All praise be yours, My Lord, for Brother Fire by whom you brighten the night. How beautiful he is, how gay, robust and strong!

All praise be yours, My Lord, for Sister Earth, our mother who feeds us, rules us and produces all sorts of fruit and coloured flowers and herbs.

All praise be yours, my Lord, for those who forgive one another for love of you and endure infirmity and tribulation. Happy are those who endure these in peace for by you, Most High, they will be crowned.

All praise be yours, My Lord, for our Sister Physical Death from whose embrace no mortal can escape, Woe to those who die in mortal sin! Happy are those she finds doing your most holy will! The second death can do no harm to them.

Praise and bless my Lord and give him thanks and serve him with great humility.

The way out of the Hermitage is back along the path but instead of going back past St Francis' Grotto you exit via the stairs and up past the Magdalen chapel and then rejoin the path you came along originally from the entrance.

Opening Times

6.30am–6.00pm (later in the Summer)
Mass is celebrated on Sundays at 8.00am and 11.00am, and 7.30am daily (also 11.00am during June, July and August). Lauds and Vespers are said daily.

Facilities

There are public toilets situated within the Hermitage domain, and are signposted off the main path before you reach the courtyard.

There is a small souvenir shop just outside the main gates but this is the only one.

San Damiano

San Damiano occupies a pivotal place in the lives of both St Francis and St Clare and a visit here is essential to understand Francis' calling and how his vow of poverty so influenced Clare and led to the foundation of a revolutionary women's order.

Entrance to San Damiano

Access

San Damiano is easily reached by foot from the centre of Assisi yet appears quite cut off from it in a rural setting, which contributes to its charm and appeal. The easiest way of getting there is to walk past the Basilica of Santa Chiara to the Porta Nuova gate, you go through it and on your right you take the escalator or stairs down to the car park. On the other side of the car park is a path that passes underneath the road and you simply continue along here through the olive groves, alongside the convent walls and come to the terrace in front of the church. (Please bear in mind that it is downhill all the way there but quite a steep walk back, anyone with walking difficulties would be advised to go by taxi.)

Alternatively you can come by car taking the main road up from the San Pietro car park and turn right down from Porta Nuova and take the left turn (signposted) to San Damiano, the convent is a short walk on the flat from the car park.

A taxi will quite happily take you for a modest fee and as mentioned in the section on the Hermitage can easily be combined with a visit there.

History

A small church existed on this site from the early eleventh century which by the time Francis knew it was under the charge of the cathedral of San Rufino. The problem of church maintenance is nothing new, the very fact that Francis found three churches to repair in a small area indicates the extent of the problem at this time. After Francis returned from his imprisonment following Assisi's war against neigbouring Perugia in 1203 he was not the same focused young man as he had been previously. He was no longer content with the same diversions or ambitions, although he was not sure where his future lay. Wandering the countryside around Assisi Francis seems to have sought out quiet places to try and 'find himself' and it was in the church of San Damiano that Francis was sure he had received a clear message from God, from the crucifix no less. Francis felt that God said to him: 'Francis, do you not see that my house is falling into ruin? Go and repair it for me.'

Francis interpreted this in the only way he knew how, literally, and immediately wanted to start renovating the church. In retrospect this message was translated as a sign that the Church needed the great evangelizing zeal of Francis at a time when the Church was engaged in a struggle against heresy and its own state of lassitude. Indeed in the fresco cycle in the Upper Basilica of St Francis you will see a scene which portrays Pope Innocent III dreaming of Francis holding up a church, thus echoing this same idea. The incident at San Damiano prompted Francis into action, he took some of the precious cloth from his father's shop and sold it, offering the proceeds to the priest at San Damiano, who promptly refused it not wanting to incur anyone's anger. However, Francis was not to be deterred and he left the money in a niche at the chapel and in spite of having to reject his own father he continued in his quest to restore the church by begging for the materials.

The restoration was completed and six years later in 1212 became the home for Clare and her followers, so that they could follow a religious life which no other foundation offered at that time. Further work was carried out at San Damiano to provide the necessary community buildings for Clare and her Sisters and there they stayed until Clare's death in 1253 when it was thought too isolated a place to remain and San Damiano was exchanged with the canons of San Rufino for the chapel of

San Giorgio (see section on Basilica of St Clare). The crucifix which had spoken to Francis went with the sisters and has had a permanent home in the Basilica of St Clare since it was built.

San Damiano continued to be occupied by Franciscan friars up until 1860 when, following the unification of North and Central Italy, ecclesiastical property was abolished and given over to the state but the property was subsequently sold to Lord Robinson, Marquis of Ripon and Viceroy of the Indies in 1879. Lord Robinson allowed a community of the Franciscan order of Observant Minors to return and also on account of his friendship with the Catholic Lothian family bequeathed San Damiano to them and in turn Lord Peter Kerr, Marquis of Lothian, returned it to the friars on the understanding this place was always dedicated to prayer and peace. A small Franciscan community is present here and the office and mass are said daily. It can be quite a lovely experience to attend Vespers here (5.00pm in winter and 7.00pm in summer) and appreciate San Damiano in a quiet and prayerful mood against the background of twilight.

Tour

The Church of San Damiano

Stand in front of the church and enter through the door on the right into a bare chapel dedicated to St Jerome with its frescoes by Tiberio D'Assisi (sixteenth century) of the Virgin Mary enthroned surrounded by saints. Follow on into the Chapel of the Crucifix and then a door on the left leads you into the church proper. Take in the simplicity of this small church and its lack of decoration but at the same time dominated by the crucifix hanging in front of you, which although a copy of the one St Francis first saw leaves you in no doubt of how impressive this sight could have appeared to one who was in such mental and spiritual turmoil. The church recently underwent a long period of restoration and has been most sympathetically renovated bringing back to life the original detail and painting, so that we now see it at its simple best.

Consider sitting here for a few minutes. A suitable prayer to say is that which Francis himself is said to have said (see section on Basilica of St Clare) or the words of Clare taken from a letter to her friend Agnes of Prague advising her about contemplating the suffering Christ on the crucifix:

> *Gaze upon,*
> *consider,*
> *contemplate,*
> *as you desire to imitate.*
> *If you suffer with him, you will*
> *   reign with Him.*
> *Weep, you shall rejoice with*
> *   Him;*
> *die with Him on the cross of*
> *   tribulation,*

you shall possess heavenly
mansions in the splendour of
the saints
and in the book of Life your
name shall be called
glorious among men.

Before proceeding into the apse of the church, go to the back and at the right of the main door is a niche known as the, 'window of the money', which was where Francis left the money for the restoration of San Damiano when the priest refused to accept it. Fourteenth-century frescoes above record this incident.

Walk up the aisle into the apse and look at the choir that still serves the community today, an inscription above the stalls dating from 1504 recalls in Latin what the true purpose of worship should be: 'not voice but desire, not noise but love, not instruments but hearts singing in the ears of God'. Above you in the vault is a fresco (thirteenth century) depicting Our Lady between Saint Rufino and Saint Damiano and at the back of the choir is a window which connected the church with the choir of Clare's community and it was through this opening that Clare and her sisters were able to venerate Francis' dead body as it was brought up from Santa Maria degli Angeli to Assisi.

Clare's convent

Leave the church through the door on the right of the altar and you are in the area which was originally the burial place of the Poor Clares and to the left of this is the *coretto* (the choir). This was a room at the centre of the community, around which the daily life of the sisters revolved, for here they would say the prayers of the office along the lines that St Benedict had originally laid down. Look into the choir across the cordon and notice the stalls and lectern both of which are thought to date from the time of Clare, they could not be simpler or more crude and are a poignant indication of the extent to which poverty was lived out here. Poverty as understood by Clare and Francis was, however, not a means of denial but of liberation, of putting oneself in a position where nothing would prevent you from meeting Christ. Clare herself spoke of the privilege of poverty and this belief was enshrined in the rule of the order.

Climb the narrow stairs, noticing about halfway up on your right a small window leading out onto a terrace, grandly called the *giardinetto* (little garden) of St Clare. By tradition this is the place that St Francis composed his 'Canticle of the Creatures' while he was spending time at San Damiano recuperating after an attempted operation to cure his eye problems by cauterization. Reaching the first floor you come into a room called St Clare's Oratory, which served as a prayer room next to the dormitory and in the niche to

Clare's New Order for Women

Clare and her followers lived a life similar to other female religious orders of the time but with some important differences. At San Damiano everyone was equal in their poverty unlike other convents, where there was a strict hierarchy depending on one's social background. Clare had insisted from the start that she would follow Francis' example as closely as possible and she resisted all attempts (even from the pope himself) to get her to accept some means of income such as property for her community. Although there was no possibility of women religious living anything other than an enclosed life, Clare would not allow any comfort, however frugal, or any security. She and her sisters depended on charity and in return were actively involved in a vocation of prayer for those outside and practical activities such as vestment-making to help restore dignity to the church which they loved so faithfully. Clare was always considered 'mother' of her community but she had no privileges and always interested herself in the well-being of her fellow sisters, offering them help and encouragement whenever needed.

the left of the altar would have been kept the convent's great treasure, the Blessed Sacrament. The sisters may not have been able to hear mass very regularly but with Christ among them in this form, they had a real focus for their prayer life. The frescoes that we now see are quite decorative but these were added after Clare's time, as we can see her and Francis clearly depicted as saints in the paintings in the apse. On the wall next to the apse is a fresco depicting Clare as protectress of her sisters and this recalls a well-chronicled event, when Clare displayed the Blessed Sacrament in its monstrance to an audience of invading Saracen forces under the command of Frederick Barbarossa. Assisi still celebrates being saved by the intercession of St Clare, on 22 June every year.

The dormitory

Up three steps you enter a large almost empty chamber, which served as the sleeping quarters for Clare's community. There was no privacy nor preference here, each sister would have had a mattress probably made of straw placed directly on the bare floor, the wind, ice and snow would have had free access, so this was literally just a roof over their heads. As you enter the room look towards the wall with the cross mounted on it and a vase of flowers or plant underneath it, this marks the place where Clare died on 11 August 1253. Clare had been bed-ridden for many years before her death and on the occasion of one Christmas because of her illness she was unable to go with the sisters to celebrate the feast in San Francesco and was depressed at not being able to join them. She received deep consolation, however, by suddenly feeling totally at one with her community, hearing the chanting and even seeing the manger. It is as a result of this 'tele-visual' experience that Clare was proclaimed patron saint of television in the 1980s!

The cloister and refectory

Pass through the door at the end of the dormitory down the steps Clare and her sisters would have walked down to observe their office in the choir at many times during the night and day. Photographs on the wall at the top of the stairs picture relics of St Clare and the order, which are now kept in private. At the bottom of the stairs you enter directly into the cloister which during Clare's time would not have the covered walkway you see now but the rooms leading off from this area are as they would have been. The refectory is in its original state with the benches

and tables that Clare and her sisters would have known and the strict command to silence painted on the walls, flowers indicate the place that Clare sat at. Frescoes on the opposite wall show a famous episode from Clare's life, remembering a visit to San Damiano by Pope Gregory IX when he took the unusual step of inviting her to bless the bread, which resulted in crosses appearing on the loaves. Back in the cloister at the corner just past the refectory is an early sixteenth-century fresco which compares Francis' stigmata with the annunciation, making a link between Mary's unconditional acceptance of God's will when she agrees to be the mother of the son of God and Francis agreeing to whatever was asked of him.

Opening Times

10.00am–12.00 and 2.00–6.00pm (4.30pm in winter)
Vespers are at 5.00pm (7.00pm in summer)
Mass is celebrated daily at 7.15am also 9.30am on Sundays and holy days of obligation.

Facilities

There are toilets in the car park.

Santa Maria degli Angeli

At first glance Santa Maria degli Angeli (Our Lady of the Angels) is a rather unremarkable suburb of Assisi down in the valley below the sparkling city, with little to mark it out except the imposing dome of the sixteenth-century basilica. However, the souvenir stalls, hotels and relatively modern church obscure the place that was the heart of Francis' evangelical mission, what he called the 'caput et mater' (head and mother) of the Friars Minor and it is here and at Rivotorto that you get a sense of the motivation and aim of Francis and his brothers.

Access

Santa Maria degli Angeli is situated about four kilometres below Assisi. Buses leave Assisi (from Piazza Matteotti, Porta Nuova and San Pietro car park) twice an hour, or alternatively take a taxi from outside the Basilica of St Clare or from the San Pietro car park below the Basilica of St Francis.

History

This area below Assisi was at the time of Francis a thickly wooded area with few inhabitants or buildings except a small church owned by the Benedictine monastery of San Benedetto at the top of Monte Subasio. This little church, also known as the Porziuncula ('little portion' because of the small plot of land it was built on) was in a rundown state like so many churches at the time. Francis had visited this church while roaming the area and felt drawn to repair this one among others after receiving the message from the crucifix in San Damiano. Although Francis had no intention of settling his brothers in one place or community, he knew that it was necessary to have a centre; and after the pope had verbally approved his Rule in 1209 the brothers were without a base having been evicted from Rivotorto and were looking for somewhere else in the vicinity. There was no easy solution to this problem as Francis and his followers were still regarded with suspicion as not being part of the established and recognized orders. Francis was quick to see that using the property of one of the orders or the secular church would be tantamount to being affiliated to them and subject to their authority. In the end he did accept the offer of the Benedictines to occupy their little church in Santa Maria degli Angeli but on a strict business footing – the church was to be rented and the Benedictines would receive an annual rent of fish in return!

The Porzinuncula was always very dear to Francis because of its dedication to Our Lady to whom he was devoted and it was here that he insisted on being brought when he was dying in 1226. Although after his death his body was transferred to Assisi, Santa Maria degli Angeli became a great place of pilgrimage and after the Council of Trent in 1568 it was decided that in order to encourage these acts of devotion a large church should be placed over the original church and the place where Francis died, which is what we see now. In 1852 earthquakes caused the façade and nave ceiling to collapse but fortunately the dome stayed intact and the building was repaired. The recent earthquakes also took their toll on the basilica, but extensive renovations were carried out afterwards and it is now completely restored.

Façade

The exterior of the basilica, though impressive, is intended to be a fitting shell for what lies inside and is therefore comparatively plain but relieved by a gold-leafed statue of the Madonna which is placed on top of the tympanum. In 1948 it was said that the statue had moved attracting huge crowds, in fact the statue did have to be physically moved in 1997 after the earthquake as it was in danger of toppling over! The enforced descent presented the opportunity for a complete

renovation of the statue, which was returned to its former position looking better than ever.

The scene surrounding you as you stand in the porch of the church is a tranquil one, with the park-like approach up to the basilica, but try and imagine the area where you are now standing occupied by crowds of up to 5,000 gathered here, including St Dominic. This is reportedly what happened in 1217 or 1219 when the so-called 'Chapter of the Mats' (mats refers to the temporary accommodation made out of branches) took place.

The Porziuncula Chapel

The purpose of the outer casing of the large basilica becomes clear when you enter it, as all your attention is naturally drawn to the humble little church which stands on its own right in the middle. The chapel is a very simple building but the sight of it is quite moving surrounded by all this open space. The frescoes on the exterior are nineteenth century replacing earlier ones and the statue niche on top was substituted for the bell tower damaged by the 1852 earthquake. In spite of the recent date of the paintings the message written just above the door is an original one: Haec est porta vitae eternae – This is the gate of eternal life.

Proceeding through the main door you are struck by the

The Porziuncula Chapel inside the Basilica of
Santa Maria degli Angeli

peace of this place and the need to be reverent, there is certainly no temptation to talk. Look at the wooden panel on the altar wall, now beautifully restored. This work was commissioned in the late fourteenth century from a painter known as Ilario di Viterbo to highlight the importance of Santa Maria degli Angeli in the work of St Francis. The upper half of the painting is taken up by a representation of St Francis being granted the Pardon (explanation below) by Christ and Our Lady. Below in the centre is the Annunciation. To the left, the upper scene is Pope Honorius granting the indulgence to Francis and beneath is Francis and the seven bishops of Umbria proclaiming the indulgence to the people. Move over to the right and in the upper section you will see a scene portraying two angels taking Francis to the Porziuncula and below it Francis being tempted by the devil.

A fitting prayer to be said in this place would be the short 'Greeting to the Blessed Virgin' by St Francis which links the two dedications of this church to Mary the Mother of God and the pardon for our sins that comes from God alone.

O holy Mother,
sweet and fair to see,
for us beseech the King,
your dearest Son,
Our Lord Jesus Christ,
to death for us delivered:
that in his pitying clemency
and by virtue of his most holy
incarnation
and bitter death
he may pardon our sins.

The exit from the chapel is on the right of the altar but do not hurry away too quickly, pay attention to the outside wall – on the right as you come out is a stone tablet marking the site below the tomb of Peter Cattani, he was Francis' beloved disciple who became the leader of the order after Francis stepped down in 1218 or 1220. However, Peter only held this office for a short time for as the plaque shows he died on 10 March 1221, five years before Francis.

The Chapel of the Transitus

If you walk forward towards the high altar of the newer church on the right you will see a small chapel, which if you did not know it was there would be easy to pass by. This is the Chapel of the Transitus and is on the site of what formed the rudimentary infirmary of Francis' original community and where the saint died. It is hard to imagine what it must have been like but it certainly did not provide much in the way of great comfort. Francis had begged to be brought here and it was in this place that his

illness finally got the better of him on the evening of 3 October 1226. After he was canonized the date of 4 October was chosen as Francis' feast day because in the monastic tradition after sundown counts as the beginning of the new day.

Through the iron grill you can see a stone which states that Francis died here and in a niche is a particularly poignant (and unusually in white only) terracotta statue of St Francis by Andrea della Robbia. There are also some relics of the saint preserved here too including the rope belt or cingulum, that Francis tied around his waist. As you stand here consider this excerpt from the biography of Francis by Thomas of Celano:

Exhausted by a severe illness, which was about to put an end to all his suffering, he had himself placed naked on the barren ground . . . Placed thus on the ground and without his canvas, he turned his face toward the sky as he usually did. With his look directed to the glory of God, he covered the wound on his right side with his left hand, not to let it be seen. He then told the friars, 'I have done my duty; may the Lord show you what you are to do.'

The Rose Garden

After you have seen the Chapel of the Transito turn back into the nave and left into the transept where you will see a sign directing you to the Rose

The Pardon of Assisi

Throughout Francis' life he was constantly wracked by notions of his own sinfulness and unworthiness and quite understandably he went through periods of doubt and human temptation. This was never more acutely demonstrated than in 1216 after the sudden death of Pope Innocent III whom Francis greatly admired, respected and was very fond of. In a fit of uncertainty and what we might perhaps call depression, Francis' thoughts turned to a life he could have led, warmed by the security and affection of a wife and children. Realizing what he had allowed himself to dwell on he felt enormous remorse and sought to correct himself in the traditional manner through physical penance and he threw himself onto roses that were in the grounds of the Porziuncula. The roses tore at Francis' flesh causing blood to drip onto the plants and tradition has it that from then on the roses grew up thornless and a deep red colour. (The Rose Garden can still be seen today.)

After this act of contrition Francis was rewarded with a vision of Christ and the Virgin Mary. Christ asks Francis what he most desires and the saint's reply is that in this church anyone seeking forgiveness from their sins could receive it. Francis is told to go and ask the pope and this he does. This request may not appear that remarkable to us but at that time the only occasion that an indulgence could be granted like this was for those embarking on the crusades. Pope Honorius asked Francis how often he wanted this privilege granted and was met with an answer that had it come from anyone else would have shocked by its rudeness: 'I am not asking for years but for souls!' Honorius was in a quandary, to permit a permanent indulgence for all those who heard confession and took communion in the Porziuncula was unheard of, but Francis' complete and utter sincerity and authority was compelling. The curia advised permitting this favour once a year and so the Feast of the Pardon is celebrated from the evening of 1 August to the evening of 2 August. In 1966 Pope Paul VI fulfilled Francis' original intentions when he extended the indulgence to every day of the year.

Garden. As you pass down the corridor note on your left a statue of St Francis which is home to several doves, they can seem quite unreal as they have the unnerving habit of sitting perfectly still! Continue along and you will see the Rose Garden on your left (mentioned in the section 'The Pardon of Assisi' above. From the Rose Garden you enter into the small

Chapel of the Roses which St Bernardine had built and is decorated with frescoes by Tiberino d'Assisi illustrating the events concerning Francis and the Pardon. To your right as you enter is a grating behind which is the site of Francis' own grotto and in it are preserved beams from the pulpit from which Francis and the seven bishops of Umbria proclaimed the indulgence.

The way back into the main church takes you another way passing the old dispensary of the community, which stored the natural remedies and medicines produced by the brothers.

Opening Times

Open every day from 6.00am–12.30 and 2.00pm until dusk

Facilities

Public toilets are situated just outside the basilica. In the passage near the Rose Garden is a shop which sells a good range of books and religious objects.

Rivotorto

Rivotorto is situated a few kilometres from Assisi, below San Damiano. There are infrequent buses from Assisi to Rivotorto, so it would be better to take a taxi, which would wait for you and take you back to Assisi or Santa Maria degli Angeli. Alternatively you can walk to and from Santa Maria degli Angeli via the English War Cemetery and take a bus back from there.

History

Rivotorto means 'serpentine brook' and refers to the stream nearby the present-day church and convent. Apart from these buildings there is little else around but imagine in Francis' day it was even more isolated and desolate, surrounded by woods. Francis and his first brothers, Bernardo di Quintavalle and Peter Catanii, found this spot with its small hut (tugurio) and felt it to be suitable to be the centre of their small community. In 1209, the year after their arrival here, Francis decided to go to Rome to gain the approval for their way of life from Pope Innocent III. This permission having been obtained the brothers returned to Rivotorto only to find that things did not always go smoothly! One day a peasant came with his donkey and marched straight in with his beast, claiming the hovel as his

own. Francis gave no objection and calmly left to look for alternative accommodation, this quest finally taking them to the Porziuncula at Santa Maria degli Angeli.

Tour

Exterior

The church that you see now dates from the second half of the nineteenth century after the earthquake that so badly damaged the basilica in Santa Maria degli Angeli, but there has been a church here since the fifteenth century. The purpose of the church was to protect the site of Francis' first community building and make it one of the shrines to be visited by the pilgrim.

On the façade of the church you see two scenes which portray two events in the life of the saint which happened here: The first, also shown in the frescoes in the Upper Basilica of St Francis, is the vision of the fiery chariot; and the second is the Emperor Otto IV passing by Assisi but Francis refuses to join the crowds greeting him and stays at Rivotorto.

Interior

What we see here occupying almost all of the nave is a reconstruction of what it is thought that the 'tugurio' was like and it consists of three small rooms. One of the chambers is called St Francis' cell which has a wooden statue of the saint in it to show that it was his. The second room is a small chapel and the third is the kitchen or 'fire room' on account of tradition having it that this was where the brothers saw Francis in the hut in a burning chariot reminiscent of the apparition of the prophet Elijah in the Old Testament.

After leaving Rivotorto it is possible to visit the British War Cemetery which is very near. In 1944 this valley was the scene of a fierce rearguard action by the German forces during which there were many casualties. The cemetery is a very moving, if harrowing, tribute to the men who died here.

Opening Times
8.00am–12.00; 2–6.00pm
Apart from the car park there are no facilities here!

Sanctuaries of the
Rieti Valley

About 80 km north of Rome along the Roman road, Via Salaria and among the Sabine mountains lies the lovely plain of Rieti, which was soon identified as a destination for Francis' missionary brothers and the effect on the area has been so profound as to give it a second name, Holy Valley. A visit to the sanctuaries in this region is a delight due to their spectacular natural setting, the fact that they are very often much quieter than Assisi and because each one is quite different in character. On a more profound level each place has its own message, having played a distinct part in the development of Francis' understanding of God.

Access

The Rieti Valley is almost equidistant from Rome and Assisi, about 1½ hours by road, but difficult to reach without private transport. In the summer there is a coach tour once a week from Assisi (details available from the Tourist Information Office). It is possible to visit all four in one day but bear in mind that the sanctuaries are not all situated in close proximity and Poggio Bustone, Greccio and Fonte Colombo are situated on mountain sides and reached by steep narrow roads only.

GRECCIO – SANCTUARY OF THE NATIVITY

Background

The name of the sanctuary is taken from the village situated two kilometres away and it is believed that this derives from 'Greek', indicating that the founding fathers of this community were perhaps exiles from Greece in pre-Roman times. At the beginning of the thirteenth century it was a fairly prosperous centre, overlooked by a castle fortified with walls and six towers (the castle was later destroyed by Frederick II in 1242). The sanctuary is situated over 1,000 metres up on Mount Lacerone and overlooks the Rieti plain.

St Francis and Greccio

Francis first came to the Rieti valley in 1209, after he had received verbal approval for his Rule and the existence of his community of brothers from Pope Innocent III. At that time Greccio was under threat from wolves and the vineyards had been devastated by hail. Francis built himself a very crude shelter near the top of Mount Lacerone and from here he spoke to the inhabitants of the area who were so impressed by what he said to them that they begged him not to leave.

One of those who was so moved by Francis' message was the local nobleman, Giovanni di Velita, who owned the castle in the village. Probably in order to encourage him to remain near Greccio, Giovanni offered Francis his choice of any spot on his land to build himself a more permanent base. Legend has it that Francis met a four-year-old child in the woods who invited him to throw a burning coal into the air. This Francis did and the coal flew like an arrow, landing a good mile away and set light to a wild spot. Francis took this as a sign that this was where he should make a centre for his brothers when they were preaching the good news in this area.

Christmas 1223

In the autumn of 1223 Francis was in Rome seeking approval from Pope Honorius III for the written Rule for the order of Friars Minor. Once the bull approving this had been issued, Francis made another request to the pope which concerned the celebration of Christmas. Ever since his journey to the

Holy Land when he had tried to intervene to stop the crusade, Francis had been greatly impressed by Bethlehem and the traditional site of the nativity. He had long meditated on the enormity of the incarnation and wanted to try and convey this essential truth of Christianity as vividly as possible to others. Therefore, Francis asked the pope for permission to celebrate the nativity by a representation of the events that happened in Bethlehem.

Francis returned to Greccio and told Giovanni di Velita to find a suitable place as he desired to see the birth of Jesus with his own eyes. Giovanni chose a spot near to where Francis had put up his rudimentary community building and it was to here that he brought the ox and ass, as instructed by Francis. There was only a rocky background to this stage, with no shelter overhead but this did not stop scores of people from the area coming here on Christmas Eve.

Francis, as deacon, read the gospel and preached the sermon, during which he was overcome by emotion while meditating on the image of Christ as a poor and vulnerable baby. When he pronounced the words: 'et verbum caro factus est' ('and the Word became flesh') he had the experience of really seeing the child and caressing its face. Everyone there was overwhelmed by the experience, especially Giovanni di Velita.

The Grotto

The chapel that you come into now was built over the open air site of the 1223 nativity celebrations during the second half of the thirteenth century. The frescoes date from the late fourteenth century and juxtapose the events of Christmas 1223 with the actual birth of Christ at Bethlehem. On the left we see St Francis with the faithful of Greccio (John of Velita is dressed in a red gown) and on the right is the nativity with Our Lady, the infant Jesus and a pensive Joseph.

The remains of Giovanni di Velita are buried here, a fitting tribute to this devoted follower of St Francis.

Original sanctuary

After the grotto you pass along a corridor into a very small central area with stairs leading off to the first floor, this would have formed the 'living' area of St Francis' first community here. It is as crude as a shelter could be, using the natural surroundings of the rock face to form it, these are living quarters at their most basic and only go to highlight Francis' understanding of the gospel message. Nothing in this place could easily distract one from personal meditation and seeking God or going out into the world to spread the good news. The chimney, remains of a sink and two little tables probably date from the time of St Francis.

Continue along the passage

(one way and very narrow!) to what is called 'St Francis' chamber' marking the end of the area of the brothers' cells, measuring about 10 metres long. The stones are what the saint had to sleep on, which caused him no distress as he preferred to have only the minimum of rest, wanting to be ready during the night to pray. It is said that Giovanni di Velita brought Francis a feather pillow, as he felt that the stones were a little too extreme but Francis apparently found this even more uncomfortable and returned it!

St Bonaventure's dormitory

Proceed up the stairs and you come to the dormitory area added on to the sanctuary only forty to fifty years after St Francis' death in 1226. It is named after St Bonaventure as he was the General Minister of the order at that time. We can learn much from these quarters about the early history of the Franciscan movement. First, the order has obviously increased quite rapidly, thus indicating the great attraction of this way of life, but on the other hand this growth has meant that the ideals of St Francis have had to be tempered to some degree and there is now a look of permanence about the sanctuary, suggesting that it was impossible for all the order to be engaged in missionary work. However, in spite of the more solid appearance of this dormitory area it is still

extremely rudimentary and short on personal comfort!

The first cell on the right is reputedly that which was once occupied by St Bonaventure and then later by the great Franciscan, Bernardine of Siena.

The choir

From the dormitory we pass first through the choir, where the community gathered to say the Divine Office and still do today. The furnishings in this room – the stalls, reading stand and lamp – are all ancient and possibly the original ones.

Chapel of St Francis

This chapel was the first extension to the area below and has the honour of being the first dedicated to St Francis in the year of his canonization, 1228. The choir stalls recall that the chapel was until the late sixteenth century divided into two parts, with the laity being separated from the community. The fittings are again likely to be the original ones, the crucifix is fourteenth century. On the altar is a prayer of St Francis that is still used in Franciscan liturgy: 'Lord, we praise you in all the churches in all the world because by your holy cross, you have redeemed the world.'

Portrait of St Francis

On your way out on the right, notice a portrait of the saint. Legend has it that this was the original painted in the year before Francis' death, on the request of his great friend,

Jacopa di Settesoli but it is most likely to be a fourteenth-century copy after the original was damaged in a fire. What makes it likely that this is fairly accurate is that it depicts Francis wiping his eyes (he suffered grieviously from an affliction, possibly trachoma) rather than images of him painted after his canonization, which focus on the many episodes which attest to his sanctity. (The halo in this picture would have been added at a later date.)

Go through the shop where there is a good selection of postcards, books and souvenirs.

New church

The new church was built in 1959 and in true Franciscan style is simple in design. As you look towards the altar, note the crib made in the wall out of terracotta with wooden figures, made by Professor Venturini. At the back of the church is a nativity which lights up scenes in turn. The stained glass features three of Francis' first companions: Brothers Leo, Ruffino and Angelo, as well as St Clare, Blessed John of Parma, 'Brother' Jacopa and John of Velita.

On the gallery on the first floor (not always open) is a permanent exhibition of cribs that have come from not only Italy but from many other parts of the world.

Opening Times
Mornings 8.00am–12 midday Afternoons 3.00pm–7.00pm (maybe earlier in winter). Access

to the main church is not possible when groups are celebrating mass or there is a wedding.

Facilities
Toilets are situated in the car park. There is a well-stocked gift shop and repository in the main courtyard which sells a good range of crib figures.

POGGIO BUSTONE – SANCTUARY OF PARDON

Access

Poggio Bustone is 18 km from Rieti and is reached from the valley by a narrow winding road. The advice for reaching here is as for Greccio. The main church is easily visited by all but be advised that access to the original grotto of St Francis is only via a steep and narrow staircase.

Background

From the start Francis had no other objective in mind than to spread the good news and he made sure his followers knew that to accompany him was not to know a settled life. No sooner had he gathered a few men around him in 1208 then he led them from Assisi into unknown territory and seemingly with no clear plan of where they were going. At Poggio Bustone they were greeted enthusiastically and warmly by the people in sharp contrast to the derision and scorn which had been heaped upon them by some in their

59

own town. Francis sought out a place where they could retreat to and where he could meditate on what God required of him and a site already occupied by a hermitage over 650 metres up was found.

In this place Francis was consumed by a problem which preoccupied him most of his life: how could God ever forgive him for all the sins he had committed in his early life, for all those times that Francis thought he had rejected God. The problem was a depressing one for if there was no pardon, there was no hope, no future. However, Francis received consolation and reassurance in his solitary confinement that God bestowed his love without condition, a love that would always forgive if forgiveness was asked for. This time of retreat also let Francis consider another pressing concern, What should he do now? Being convinced of God's unerring love for us he understood that this was the message that was so badly needed by the world at large and it was from here at Poggio Bustone that the missionary work of Francis and his followers really began. Just as Christ had sent out his disciples in pairs so did Francis, although at this stage they only numbered eight in all!

Tour

From the car park enjoy the wonderful views down to the valley below and appreciate the peace of this isolated spot as this is what Francis and his

followers would have seen and been impressed by, not the church which we might notice first and was built at least 150 years after Francis' death.

Church of St James the Great

The church was built at a higher level than the hermitage that Francis used, but is still of a very simple construction. Some parts of seventeenth-century frescoes remain along with a fifteenth-century painting of the Holy Family but much of the interior decoration was damaged during an earthquake in 1948.

The convent

As you come out of the church go round to your right and you enter a small cloister which formed part of the early community buildings and comprised of a few rooms to serve as kitchen and dormitory as well as a church which with the construction of the newer church was relegated to use as a corridor. To reach the area that Francis would have known and that he used for his retreat place, you follow the path down outside the building and reach what is little more than a cave hewn from the rock, probably an ancient place of hermitage and given to Francis and his companions by the Benedictine order. This rough place was dedicated to St James, indicated by the small statue placed here. The crude simplicity of these surroundings reminds us once again of the enormous consolation and inspiration that Francis received in withdrawing from the world in this way and how much he relied upon it for reassurance.

A reflection on God's pardon and forgiveness

Thomas of Celano records in his biography of Francis that the saint liked to withdraw to a lonely place and once in the course of spending time in this way:

> *He was waiting in fear and trembling upon the ruler of the world and thinking in the bitterness of his soul about his past years ill-spent, he kept repeating the words over and over again: 'God be merciful to me a sinner.'*
>
> *This unspeakable joy began to fill his heart and the certainty was granted him that all his sins were forgiven.*

The Little Temple of Peace

After leaving the grotto head back up to the square in front of the church, just opposite here is a small monument to Francis, recently constructed out of the apse which remained of a former church. At the back is a statue that shows Francis smiling, which perhaps is not the common image of him although contemporary accounts do attest to his cheery disposition and we are reminded here of the continuous joy that experiencing God's creation gave to Francis. By the side of the archway is a plaque which

translated means: St Francis of Assisi departing from this mountain in the winter of 1209 called to himself his first seven companions and said to them: 'Go, beloved brothers, two by two through the world and announce peace to men.'

If you have time to spend here you can take the path leading up from the square in front of the church which leads to a small chapel built over the site of another of the places where Francis spent time in meditation. Be warned though, as picturesque as it is clinging to the side of the rock face it does involve a walk of about half an hour, ascending nearly 300 metres!

Opening Times
8.30am–1.00pm; 3–7.00pm

Facilities
There are no toilets here or any amenities to speak of.

FONTE COLOMBO – THE 'FRANCISCAN SINAI'

Access

General comments are the same for those concerning Greccio and Poggio Bustone as Fonte Colombo is over 500 metres above sea level and reached by a fairly narrow and winding road about 5 km from Rieti.

Background

Fonte Colombo (Spring of the Doves) takes its name from a spring which rises in the woods on the hillside and Francis would have known it by this name. Francis came to this place near the end of his life but at a crucial time for him and his brothers. From his time at Fonte Colombo came the third version of the Rule that Francis wrote to provide the framework for his order and still today structures the many Franciscan communities all over the world.

It is quite probable that Francis himself did not feel entirely at ease with the idea of having to compose a written Rule for his followers but the need arose because of the incredible numbers of men who wished to join the Friars Penitent as they were first known or Friars Minor as they were soon called. Francis, of course, desired and encouraged others to take up his challenge but at the same time he became overwhelmed by the response and the almost impossible task of organizing and administering this very disparate group. Francis had written a very simple and short First Rule in 1209–10 which was superseded in 1221 by a much longer one. However, the second version was not considered workable or practical enough to serve as an effective constitution, and he was soon urged to rethink it by the leading friars and Cardinal Ugolino (who later as Pope Gregory IX canonized Francis). Francis spent time alone at the sanctuary pondering on the contents and dictating it for Brother Leo who wrote it down.

News of Francis' composition of this Third Rule was not greeted with

enthusiasm by all his brothers for in spite of the great example shown them by their 'Father Francis', they felt that the extreme austerity practised by him could not be expected from everyone. Their anxiety made them go to Fonte Colombo to seek some reassurance that the Rule would not be too exacting and would make some compromises to help the order fit more easily into society. Francis, with his usual ability to cut to the quick, instead of responding directly to his brothers, addressed Christ directly saying that he knew that they would not believe him. According to the account in 'The Mirror of Perfection' those gathered heard a voice which said: 'Francis, nothing in this Rule is yours; for all is mine. I wish the Rule to be obeyed to the letter, without a gloss.' Whatever, the true course of events Francis as was typical of him confirmed that the Rule was not communicating his own ideas but God's, received by him through his meditations, and because of this Fonte Colombo is compared to Moses receiving the Ten Commandments on Mount Sinai. Unfortunately, the Third Rule did not stop the friars from further debating the instructions laid down by Francis, leading ultimately to a division of the order not long after his death, into the Observants, those who kept the Rule to the letter and the Conventuals who allowed compromise over such issues as the communities owning property. The original copy of the Rule is now kept in the Basilica of St Francis in Assisi.

Fonte Colombo is also significant in Francis' life as the place where doctors operated on his eyes in order to try and restore some vision and improve Francis' health, as Cardinal Ugolino and others were afraid that without his sight Francis' influence over his order would not be as effective. A trachoma infection, most likely contracted when Francis went to the Middle East could have been the cause but the only known treatment at the time, which is quite unthinkable to us without the use of anaesthetic, was to try and cauterize the veins in the sides of the eyes with a branding iron. Not unexpectedly, the brothers in attendance could not bear to be in the room as this operation was carried out but they were quite astonished to hear no reaction from Francis. Furthermore it is recorded that he upbraided them for their cowardice in running away! Whatever the reason for Francis' tremendous fortitude whether through mental strength or numb flesh, which could have resulted from previous illness, his reaction is still most impressive. Even though no improvement resulted, Francis was uplifted by the experience and it prompted him to dedicate a stanza in the Canticle of Creatures to 'Brother Fire'.

Tour

The church

Cross the Piazza and visit the church dating from the second half of the thirteenth century but later enlarged and dedicated to St Francis and St Bernardine of Siena. Inside the church there are two striking pieces of art picturing Francis: the first on the right is the saint kneeling at the foot of a crucifix, and a little further on is a depiction in wood of Christ dictating the Rule to St Francis and at the side Brother Leo writing it down. The latter was executed by a member of the Franciscan order, Brother John of Pisa.

The sanctuary

Although the church retains the simple and prayerful Franciscan atmosphere, it is behind this building that we discover the most moving reminders of Francis. As you leave the church on your right is a small archway, go down a short way and enter on the right a small chamber which was used by Francis and his companions and where the operation on his eyes took place. This room is now adjoined by extended monastery buildings which St Bernardine had constructed.

Cappella della Maddalena

In front of you as you come out of the sanctuary is a small chapel that Francis would have seen when he arrived here and which was much loved by him and here Brother Leo would have celebrated mass. Medieval frescoes including one depicting St Clare still remain, but more startling still is the 'Tau' symbol that you can see painted in an alcove to the left of the altar. The 'Tau' symbol was adopted by Francis for his symbol and is still used by the Franciscans today.

Sacro speco (holy cave)

Below the Cappella della Maddalena you can reach the cave (sacro speco) where St Francis meditated and

formulated the Rule in his mind. (Please note that access is not advised for those with any mobility problems.) Places like this were often considered holy in medieval times because they provided an image of the tomb that Christ was placed in and where he rose from the dead.

Opening Times

The main church is open from 8.00am–12.30pm and 3.00pm–7.00pm
The sanctuary and Cappella della Maddalena are open from 8.00am–7.00pm (5.00pm in winter)

T

The Symbol of the Tau

You cannot miss the Tau cross in any Franciscan place and in Assisi the little wooden versions in gift shops make their presence felt everywhere! It is not known exactly why Francis adopted this particular cross form, although as in so many areas of his religious life this form of devotion was no innovation. Certainly the simple cross form was recognized as the crucifix before the upper straight piece appeared in later medieval art. The Tau was also understood as a symbol of redemption as illustrated in the book of Ezekiel when in a vision Ezekiel sees the angel sparing from death only those who are brandished with this sign. 'Tau' was the translation of this sign in the Vulgate Bible being likened to the letter of the ancient Greek alphabet and was similar to the last letter of the Hebrew alphabet and so like Omega indicates that God is at the end of everything. It was not only Francis who felt drawn to use the Tau as his personal symbol; Pope Innocent III made the Tau the symbol of his reforms. What is obvious is the importance of the Tau to Francis as he drew the sign himself on the blessing that he wrote for Brother Leo and which today is kept at the Basilica of St Francis in Assisi.

Facilities

There are toilets here and a small repository which is sometimes open.

SANTA MARIA DELLA FORESTA – SANCTUARY OF THE MIRACLE OF THE GRAPES

Access

Santa Maria is situated about 5 km from Rieti. General information on reaching Santa Maria is as for the other Rieti Valley sanctuaries.

Background

In 1225 the year before his death Francis stayed at La Foresta for a short while before the operation on his eyes was undertaken at Fonte Colombo. At that time there was a small chapel of San Fabiano looked after by a priest, with humble accommodation attached to it. Word that Francis was staying here spread quickly and soon people were congregating at La Foresta to catch a glimpse of him, which made the priest rather anxious as he was more worried about his vineyards being trampled by the crowd than them receiving the word of God from the friar from Assisi! Francis reading the mind of the priest begged him to let him stay at La Foresta and be willing to sacrifice his grapes for Francis' sake and for the good of the people and in return the cleric would be well rewarded. The priest, amazed at Francis' telepathy and ashamed at his own selfishness agreed and in

return his vines miraculously provided a bumper crop and the best wine ever made.

Hermits moved into La Foresta in the fourteenth century and built the church of Santa Maria and were followed by a community of Clareni brothers (who later became incorporated into the Franciscan order) but now the sanctuary is owned privately.

Tour

Santa Maria della Foresta is still today surrounded by open countryside and a cultivated plot at its side helps us imagine the original scene. As you approach the sanctuary along the drive you will pass a series of ceramic Stations of the Cross which were made in the eighteenth century for the monastery of St Bonaventure in Frascati, and just in front of the entrance to the sanctuary is a ceramic depiction of the Madonna of the Grapes.

The two churches of Santa Maria and San Fabiano are situated side by side. Santa Maria dating from the fourteenth century is a simple church, plainly decorated enlivened only by the terracotta Madonna and Child behind the altar and the two modern stained glass windows which figure the hermits who had care of the sanctuary first and their benefactor Filippa Lucarelli in one and the Clareni in the other.

San Fabiano, although having been subjected to various

alterations, is in essence still the little church that Francis would have known. The painted panelled ceiling above the altar with its repeated Tau pattern reminds us of the connection with Francis even though the frescoes in the apse that remain do not mention him. The paintings dating from the fifteenth century show Christ the Saviour blessing on the outside of the arch, John the Baptist on the left and (probably) Santa Barbara, patroness of Rieti, on the right. Next to Christ we see the figure of a pope on the left and San Fabiano on the right, with St Peter in the roundel and San Ludovico underneath and on the opposite side St Paul above a Virgin and child. St Catherine and scenes from the life of Our Lady appear on the side wall.

The domus

After coming out of the churches you can go down to the area called the *domus* (from the Latin for house) which was the living area that Francis occupied during his stay here and where in a cell on a lower level he retired to pray in quiet and also to be protected from the light which so hurt his eyes. Some authorities are of the opinion that the 'Canticle of the Creatures' was written here and not at St Damiano and this is recorded in the modern marble monument outside the sanctuary. In the domus there is the original stone sink which was where the grapes were pressed.

Opening Times
8.30am–12 midday and
3.00pm–6.00pm

La Verna (Sanctuary of the Stigmata)

Access

La Verna lies within the Casentino National Park at about 70 km from Assisi by way of the E45 road turning off at Pieve Santo Stefano and following the signs. During summer months it is possible to take an organized tour from Assisi (information available from Tourist Information Office), otherwise it is difficult to reach La Verna by public transport. It should be noted that the way to La Verna is reached by a winding road which has to make its way up to height of over 1,000 m. There is a car park just outside the sanctuary gates for both cars and coaches.

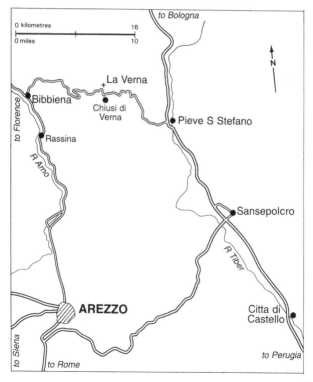

Background

La Verna is the present name of the mountain on which the sanctuary is situated, but its ancient name was Monte Alverna and this was how Francis would have known it. The history of this place began not on these slopes but further east in the province of Emilia Romagna through which in 1213 Francis was making his way to reach the coast and from there sail to Morocco and strive to achieve peace between the Christian and Muslim forces of the crusade. The brothers were passing by the great fortress of San Leo where celebrations were taking place in honour of a Count of Montefeltro who had just gained his knighthood. Never one to miss an opportunity to preach the gospel, Francis led his brothers to the castle precinct and spoke to all who would hear him, impressing many including Count Orlando of Chiusi who offered Francis some land on his estates as a place of sanctuary and hermitage. Francis promised to send some of his brothers to see the place and if it was suited to being used as a place of prayer then the offer would be gratefully taken up.

As we can now see La Verna proved itself to fit the criteria for a place well isolated from the world, offering tranquillity and few distractions. The mountain did however already have some inhabitants, robbers in fact, and Orlando provided the first Franciscans here with

an escort of fifty armed men. Legend has it though that even these robbers were won over by Francis and joined his band, their leader changing his name from 'Brother Wolf' to 'Brother Lamb' to indicate the new direction his life was taking.

Francis' stigmata

Francis had spent most of his adult life devoted to intimately following Christ step for step, identifying his experiences with those that Jesus had first lived. Like St Clare Francis meditated often on the passion and death of Christ, leaving him extremely affected and drained and it is not surprising that Francis aspired to unite his own sufferings gained through illness with those of his Lord. In 1224 Francis went up to La Verna to prepare for the Feast of the Exultation of the Cross on 14 September. We do not know why Francis should have especially chosen La Verna over any other of the sanctuaries, but he arrived here some time before the feast day and as was his custom cut himself off from the other brothers by finding his own particular spot for his contemplation. During one night Francis had a vision of a winged seraph enfolding a crucified man the sensation of which left Francis overwhelmed by a sense of being utterly invaded by the love of God. This mystical state of ecstacy was different in one remarkable aspect to previous experiences as it had inextricably united the spiritual and the physical by leaving Francis with an imprint of Christ's wounds received at his crucifixion. To all those who saw the injuries to his hands, feet and sides it was apparent there was no doubt that heaven had accorded him the highest honour.

Scholars have hotly debated the cause of Francis' wounds, some attributing them to a form of tubercular leprosy or other illness. The church itself investigated this matter after Francis' death because of the serious implications if it were held to be true, but the stigmata was confirmed by the pope and is the first record of this phenomenon which has been experienced by others throughout the centuries including St Catherine of Siena and more recently Padre Pio (the twentieth-century Franciscan brother canonized in June 2002).

A Franciscan community still resides at La Verna and many of the brothers from many parts of the world are there as part of their novitiate formation which makes for a very international atmosphere and bears witness to the universal appeal of the poor man from Assisi.

Tour

After entering the gates to the sanctuary there is about a 500-metre walk to the complex of buildings which includes the new church and the Chapel of the Stigmata but this stroll through the woods sets the scene and the tone of the place, helping to put one in a contemplative frame of mind. Keep following the straight and relatively flat path, ignoring the ones which lead further up into the woods. After a while you will see buildings and on your left signs to the bar and information office before passing through the first arch and then after the shop you pass into a small open square called the Quadrante. It is a good idea here (weather permitting) to cross the piazza to the wall opposite to enjoy the wonderful view of the valley below and to take an overview of the sanctuary domain.

As with all Francis' hermitages what we can still see today has changed much from his times and it is helpful to stop in this square and spend a few minutes imagining La Verna as it was. Where you are standing now would not have been a clearing and would have been occupied by trees the same as those you saw on your approach. To your left as you face the main church you might just have been able to make out the grottoes in the rocks that the brothers used as their cells and just a little to your right down the slope would have been the one permanent building constructed by Francis and his companions, the little church of Santa Maria degli Angeli, and it is here that you should begin your discovery of this place.

Looking up to La Verna

Chapel of Santa Maria degli Angeli

As you face the main church go down the slope to the right-hand side and in the left corner you will see doors to the church. The interior is intentionally simple and austere but all the more moving for that and one is struck by the atmosphere which demands silence without needing a notice to remind you. St Francis named this chapel himself, calling it the same as the church in Assisi that he regarded as the heart and mother of his order. The original church started where the iron grill is today, the entrance having been added in

70

1250 to accommodate the growing number of worshippers.

The simplicity and size of the chapel mean that you are immediately struck not only by the size but the beauty of the panel behind the altar by Andrea della Robbia depicting the assumption of Our Lady into heaven. Mary is seen rising above her tomb accompanied by angels, beneath her looking on are on the left St Gregory the Great and St Thomas, and on the right St Francis and St Bonaventure. Under the floor in this main part of the church Count Orlando, who gave the land of La Verna to Francis was singularly honoured by being given a burial place here.

As you leave the chapel notice the two terracotta panels by Giovanni della Robbia on each side above the metal dividing screen that represent the taking of Christ down from the cross and the nativity.

After visiting the Chapel of Santa Maria degli Angeli you can go and walk through to view the convent buildings constructed in the fifteenth

---

The della Robbia terracottas

La Verna is home to the largest collection in the world of the work of the della Robbia family. This family developed a unique form of art inspired by the enormous energy and genius of what we know as the Renaissance, using the principles of ceramics to make pictoral representations (almost all with a religious theme). The revolutionary multi-firing process and enamel varnish that was used created an extremely hardy finish which overcame the problem of the climate that often affected frescoes. Apart from the sheer technical mastery of these terracottas, they are astonishing because of the clear and moving way they convey the episodes of the gospel and in this they show the influence of the Catholic reform movement spearheaded by the Dominican Savonarola of which Botticelli and Fra Angelico were also a part. This group deplored the use of religious subjects in art merely to develop the artist's technique resulting in some madonnas looking too beautiful by half! Some of these works were commissioned by the community at La Verna itself and some were donated by families like the powerful Rucellai of Florence. The della Robbia dynasty starting with Luca continued to be involved in this field for about a hundred years until the 1520s. It is really worth taking time and sitting in the church and two chapels and just looking at the della Robbia terracottas, it is not so much the longer you concentrate on them the more you see, rather the more that you will feel moved by them.

century, which demonstrate the growth of the order and the change in character for a large part of the Franciscan movement from a nomadic lifestyle to something much more stable, and even worldly.

Basilica

From the Cappella of Santa Maria degli Angeli turn back to the square and enter the main church (begun in 1348 and finished in 1568) which was accorded the status of basilica by the pope in 1921. This church was built with funds donated by among others, the most powerful guild of Florence the Arte della Lana and reflects the enormous influence of the Franciscans in society at that time. The interior conforms with the ideals of Franciscan simplicity but is relieved by della Robbia terracottas in the side chapels:

- In the first chapel on the right is a relief of Madonna of the Refuge which was only moved to La Verna in 1874 from the oratory of Saint Onofrio, the patron saint is depicted on the far left of Our Lady.
- About halfway up the nave are two *tempietti* (little temples) and in the left one we see the most serene depiction of the Annunciation, considered to be by many the greatest work by Andrea della Robbia. Mary is shown serenely accepting the message brought by Gabriel while God the Father looks on in the right-hand

corner and the Holy Spirit represented by a dove witnesses the scene.
- In the right-hand alcove is the nativity again showing God the Father and the Holy Spirit as spectators. Especially appealing about this scene is the look on the faces of the angels and cherubim who are obviously moved by this great event.
- On either side of the entrance to the high altar are two of the principal figures of the Franciscan movement: St Francis on the left and St Anthony Abbot on the right.
- In the chapel to the left of the main altar (called the Ridolfi chapel after the family who sponsored it) is the ascension. Christ rises from this earth, signified by the trees and hills, as his apostles and mother look up towards him.

As you come out of the church do not miss on your left a side chapel near the entrance where relics of St Francis are displayed including a blood-stained piece of cloth which covered Francis' side after he had received the stigmata. Also enclosed are items which the saint used while staying with Count Orlando: a cup, tablecloth and bowl and personal items such as part of a tunic cord, a stick and iron scourging instrument.

The corridor of the stigmata

Once back in the square you will see a covered corridor

leading off to your right. Francis probably would not have approved of this addition to the sanctuary which was added in 1573 to allow the brothers to process to the Chapel of the Stigmata in all weathers without any ill effect! Don't be tempted to pass down the corridor too quickly and miss the frescoes on the wall which date from the seventeenth century and depict many of the pivotal events from Francis' life and make a fitting preparation for the Stigmata Chapel at the end.

Halfway up the corridor on the right is an entrance to stairs leading down to the cave Francis used as his own cell and as usual there is no concession to creature comforts. (*This visit is not recommended for those who find walking down steep steps difficult.*)

At the end of the corridor you will see on the left the entrance into a small chapel dedicated to St Anthony of Padua who spent several months here before his death in 1231 only five years after that of Francis. Going out of here by the other door you come out onto a precipice which shows the dramatic rock formation on which La Verna is built, which tradition has it was caused at the time of the crucifixion of Christ.

Chapel of the Stigmata

Before you enter this chapel remember that Francis did not know this building which was built in 1263 after his death.

What he would have seen was a rocky outcrop, a lonely spot which he chose merely as an isolated place suitable for the most intense devotions and the only shelter would have been made of the materials nature provided.

The immediate focus of this chapel is the Andrea della Robbia crucifixion behind the altar, but your attention should first turn to the roped off feature in the centre of the nave which is the rock where tradition has it was the place where Francis devoted himself entirely to his Lord in the deepest prayer and contemplation and was granted the ultimate honour of receiving the wounds of the stigmata. However, even in this desolate spot Francis was comforted by nature in the form of a falcon who kept him company and woke him from sleep to remind him of the time for matins by singing and beating his wings.

A prayer which could aid meditation in this holy place is one not written by St Francis but which he included in his own devotions:

> *May the burning and tender*
> *   might*
> *of your love,*
> *I beseech you, O Lord,*
> *ravish my soul*
> *from all earthly things:*
> *so that I may die*
> *for love of my love.*

The crucifixion by Andrea della Robbia is a most fitting

complement to this place and was designed specifically for it having been commissioned by the Alessandri family of Florence who are remembered by their family emblem being included on both sides of the inscription at the bottom. The scene is one of profound grief with even the sun and moon making obvious their sorrow. The air of desolation is expressed by the figures at the foot of the cross, on the left Our Lady and St Francis, on the right St John and St Jerome (on whose feast day Francis left La Verna for the last time). Death, however, does not have the last word for the skull is relegated to a place under the cross, indicating that Christ has triumphed over death.

Before you leave this chapel notice also the lovely wooden choir stalls dating from the fifteenth century and lovingly restored in the 1890s by the sacristan, Brother Galimberti. The popes and men who feature in the inlaid panels are those who at some time have confirmed their belief in St Francis' stigmata.

Chapel of St Mary Magdalen and the Projecting Rock

Before you get back to the square by the basilica on your right you will see a small chapel (not always open unfortunately) dedicated to St Mary Magdalen which has been built over the site of

Francis' first cell here in the place that Count Orlando had a shelter set up in 1214. The altar stone served as Francis' table and it was here that it is claimed Christ appeared to the saint and they had many conversations.

Descending down a steep path (*not recommended for those with walking difficulties*), you come to the Sasso Spicco a mass of stone that juts out from the rock face and was the place where Francis spent much time meditating on the passion of Our Lord. In fact Francis made a point of including the Sasso Spicco in his farewell to La Verna which he thanked for having protected him from the temptation of the devil.

Opening Times
The sanctuary is open every day from early morning until evening. Religious services are a continuous feature of La Verna's large Franciscan community including daily mass at 11.00am and a procession to the Stigmata Chapel each day after vespers in the basilica at 3.00pm to commemorate Francis receiving the stigmata. Participation in the procession can really help make a visit to La Verna a very special part of one's pilgrimage to the Franciscan sanctuaries.

Facilities
La Verna often sees hundreds of visitors in one day at the weekend and on feast days and so is well prepared to cater for them. As you enter the sanctuary complex there is the *refetorio*

(restaurant) and also the information office, toilets and bar, near to the chapel of Santa Maria degli Angeli there are more toilets. A very good shop (just after the main entrance to the sanctuary) sells not only guide books, postcards and religious objects but also a range of natural cosmetics and foodstuffs made at La Verna, which are displayed in the room which was the old pharmacy. The shop is open until 12.00 midday, from 1.30–2.45pm and from after the procession until 6.00pm.

Just by the car park at the entrance to the sanctuary is another restaurant and bar 'La Melosa' which offers very good regional food at modest prices.

Feast days at La Verna

15 August Assumption of Our Lady and titular feast of the basilica

17 September Stigmata of St Francis

Celebrations begin on the eve of the feast days.

As you leave La Verna it is a good time to consider the words of St Francis to Brother Leo as he left La Verna for the last time:

The Lord bless you and keep you and
turn his countenance upon you.
The Lord have mercy on you and grant you his peace.
The Lord give you his holy blessing.

Gubbio

Francis spent eighteen years of his life working to spread the word of the gospel but within that short time the communities of his brotherhood mushroomed all over Italy and into Europe in a way that no other religious order had ever done before. Francis himself was continuously on the move setting up and visiting many of the centres which were not only used as a base from where to preach the good news to all people, but also as a place for meditation and reflection. Just looking at a map of the various sanctuaries in the regions of Umbria and Tuscany alone will astonish you by the number that there were, many of them still in existence. Although it makes sense to concentrate any visit to the Franciscan places on those which help us understand Francis' message such as those in Assisi, the Rieti Valley and La Verna, if time permits discovering one or two others can only help us gain a clearer picture of the impact that Francis had on the world that he lived in. In addition these spots will introduce you to some lovely and quite unspoilt parts of Italy that otherwise you would never have found.

GUBBIO

Gubbio was a flourishing city at the time of Francis and one that he knew through the cloth trade and where he had good friends. It must have been an impressive sight then and still is very much so today with its massive stone structures that have you craning your neck upwards to take them all in as you walk through the streets. Even if it were not for the Franciscan connection omitting a visit to Gubbio if you come to Umbria would be a grave mistake. Gubbio can easily be the subject of a book in itself so included here are details of those places with a particular memory of St Francis and a few hints about other places to see. The visitor is highly recommended to buy a guide book on arrival or use one of those listed in the bibliography at the end of this book.

Access

By road Gubbio is about one and a half hour's drive from Assisi, the distance is not that great and neither are the roads. There is no station at Gubbio but it is possible to travel from Assisi to Fossato di Vico by train from where there is a connecting bus to Gubbio and this takes about two hours. (You can obtain details from the Tourist Information Office in Assisi.) Gubbio really deserves a whole day and as there are some very good restaurants serving regional

View of the Palazzo dei Consoli, Gubbio

cuisine, there is no reason to cut short your visit.

Background

Gubbio (for most people who have a knowledge of Francis' life) immediately conjures up images of the story of the wolf but in fact Francis' association with the place must have begun in his youth as it was to a family in this town that he came for shelter at the very beginning of his missionary period. Having cut himself off from his family Francis walked away from Assisi still on the quest for his path in life. After having begged for aid from a monastery he carried on to Gubbio and his friends, the Spadalonga family and in particular the son, Federico. In spite of the great change that the family must have seen in their friend, they did not desert him and showed far more Christian charity than the monks had done. It is recorded that the family gave Francis hospitality and a new tunic and later contributed to funds for a church for the Friars Minor. Today we can see remains of the Spadalonga property in the Church of San Francesco (see below). In Gubbio St Francis continued his work with lepers that had started in Assisi and the brothers who came to settle in Gubbio were directed by Francis to make the care of the leper community the focus of their ministry.

Gubbio in the thirteenth century was surrounded by forests inhabited by wild animals and at one time tradition has it was terrorized by a wolf probably starving and in search of food. Francis who only saw God in all aspects of the world around him treated the wolf as a person and appealed to him to stop terrifying the people and in return he would be fed. The wolf impressed by the saint held out his paw to confirm the agreement. This event is remembered in two churches, San Francesco della Pace in the centre of town and La Vittorina just outside. After Francis' death his Friars Minor continued to be a great influence in the city and the Church of St Francis is still today one of the major features of the skyline.

Tour

Church of San Francesco

(Situated in the lower part of the town near the main parking area.) This church in typical austere and plain Franciscan style was built in the mid-thirteenth century near the site of the Spadalonga family house and warehouse. Traces of the house can be seen in the Capella di San Francesco in the right apse and also in the sacristy. Of great interest is the fresco cycle of the Life of Mary by the fifteenth-century Gubbio artist, Ottaviano Nelli.

San Francesco della Pace

Easy to walk past without paying it much attention, this little church near to the city centre and the Palazzo del Popolo was constructed in the seventeenth century to remember the place where tradition has it the wolf (once tamed by St Francis) used to come at night to take shelter. Inside the church the statue above the altar reminds you that this place is associated with the story of the wolf. But if you are in any doubt look at the tomb by the side of the altar under which in 1872–3 excavations claimed to have found the skeleton of a wolf and although its origin cannot be authenticated it provides a convenient alibi for tradition. The altar stone itself is also held to be part of this tale as it is claimed to be the stone upon which Francis preached reconciliation between the citizens of Gubbio and the wolf. Whatever the precise details, the moral of this incident is very clear and one very much in tune with Francis' mission to convert all God's kingdom to the message of peace brought by Christ.

La vittorina

Just a little way out of the town taking Viale della Vittoria in the lower part of the city you can reach the little church called the Vittorina, which some claim takes its name from a victory over the Saracens and others from the ancient name of the place, Vehia Turena. The derivation is irrelevant however to the Franciscan link which is that this place was given to the friars by the Bishop of Gubbio in 1213 and became their first base in Gubbio from where they went out to work in the leper house. The church shows little of its earliest origins though it retains the simple and modest appearance which would have suited the Franciscan ideals. In front of the church there is a statue which again reminds us of the wolf as this is the place which tradition records as being the spot where Francis encountered the wolf.

Other places of interest in Gubbio

Gubbio is one of the richest cities in Umbria in terms of historical heritage also benefiting from its beautiful setting, lying at the foot of Mount Ingino. Below are just a few suggestions of what could be seen in a day as well as the above.

Palazzo dei Consoli and Palazzo del Popolo

In the centre of the town you cannot miss the mass of stone that makes up these two awesome fourteenth-century public buildings which were built to demonstrate the might and wealth of Gubbio, the sheer scale of them is quite overwhelming. A visit inside (entrance fee payable) is recommended if for one reason alone – to see the Eugubian Tablets, bronze plaques dating from the second century BC which, written partly in the ancient Umbrian language and partly in Latin, reveal much about the people in this area at the time and provide the key to deciphering Etruscan script.

The cathedral (duomo)

Behind the Palazzo dei Consoli going uphill the cathedral is slightly obscured but no less of a treasure. Built at the end of the twelfth century it is like many Romanesque churches understated on the outside, but the interior with its very fine stone vaulting and works of art in the side chapels is well worth the visit.

Palazzo Ducale

Just opposite the cathedral is the palace erected by the powerful Montefeltro family who at one time governed a large swathe of this part of the country. In spite of a lack of furniture this is still an extremely fine example of a Renaissance palace with all the intricacy and elegance one would expect, which is evident particularly in the courtyard, the staircase and the interior architectural detail.

The sanctuary of St Ubaldo

High above the city (827 metres) the sanctuary dedicated to Gubbio's most famous bishop, Ubaldo, looks down on and watches over his people. Ubaldo was known for his exemplary life devoted to poverty and also his care for his native town which he showed by negotiating for its independence with the emperor, Frederick Barbarossa, and encouraging the

reconstruction of the city after a devastating fire. After his death in 1160 his remains were brought up the mountain to an ancient place of pilgrimage and the shrine has since been a place of devotion of which the Franciscan order is now the custodian. You may well notice some rather odd looking wooden constructions kept in the church a little like huge pencils. These are the Ceri (candles) and are carried by representatives of their ancient guilds in a race from the town to the top of the hill as part of the festivities in May each year to celebrate the feast of St Ubaldo.

A visit to the shrine of St Ubaldo is interesting for several reasons: the view from above is wonderful, the sanctuary is a very prayerful and peaceful place and getting up there gives you the chance to try out one of the most interesting forms of transport there is. The 'funivia' is no ordinary cable car as the compartments are like large baskets that you stand in and have to jump in and out of to get on and off because the mechanism goes round continuously. You can reach the funivia by going out of the Porta Romana, signs in the town will show you the way and rest assured that it is worth it for the view over the city coming down.

Opening Times

Sanctuary of St Ubaldo 9.30am–1.00pm and 3.30–7.00pm. Closed on Monday throughout the year. Entrance fee payable The cathedral and other churches are usually open daily in the morning and afternoon but closed between midday and 3.00pm. The Church of San Francesco was at the time of writing closed, please enquire at the Tourist Information Office for further details.

The cable car operates all year round 10.00am–1.15pm and 2.30pm–5.00pm (not Wednesdays in winter). In July and August it goes non-stop all day from 8.30am until 7.30pm

The Palazzo dei Consoli is open from 10.00am–1.00pm and 2.00pm–5.00pm (entrance fee)

The Palazzo Ducale is open from 9.00am–1.00pm and 2.30pm–7.00pm (entrance fee)

Sanctuary of Le Celle and Cortona

Cortona is one of the loveliest and most interesting cities of southern Tuscany and within a short distance from it you will find the enchanting sanctuary of Le Celle which is a living testament to the spirit of St Francis.

Access

Cortona is situated just inside Tuscany and can be reached in little more than an hour by road from Assisi via Perugia. Alternatively you could take a train from Assisi towards Florence alight at Terontola and take a bus for the remaining 10 km. The sanctuary of Le Celle is situated about 3.5 km outside the town and reached along a narrow and winding road, signs direct you from Cortona.

SANCTUARY OF LE CELLE

Le Celle is one of the most picturesque of the sanctuaries originally founded by St Francis and without a doubt has a very special and evocative atmosphere. Although it is much visited by tourists and religious alike, it still conveys a wonderful sense of peace surrounded by nature just as when Francis first came here in 1211.

Background

Francis first came to Cortona shortly after having gained permission from the pope to preach and form a community. He was probably accompanied by Silvester who had been a priest at the Cathedral of San Rufino in Assisi, but as elsewhere, Francis' magnetism soon attracted others including a young man from Cortona called Guido (later beatified and known as Blessed Guido). Some believe that Guido was in fact the author of the 'Little Flowers', the collection of episodes of Francis' life. What attracted Francis to Le Celle is obvious as it offered seclusion, peace and a naturally beautiful setting. It is likely that as was the case with other locations selected for a sanctuary there were already buildings here as suggested in the name of Le Celle (the cells) and it is possible that this referred to buildings used as water mills. After Francis died Le Celle still served as a hermitage for a while and Brother Elias, the Minister General of the order stayed here as well as St Anthony of Padua. But with the growth of the Franciscan order and preference by many brothers to move into large complexes in towns, Le Celle fell into disuse for a while. In fact you can see the result of the Conventual Franciscan development in Cortona itself in the Church of San Francesco and its adjacent monastery which was founded by Elias.

It took another three hundred years before the Franciscans were reassociated with Le Celle and this was thanks to a reforming group founded in the sixteenth century and called the Friars of the Eremetical Life, more usually known as Capuchins on account of the pointed hood that they wore. The Capuchins were responsible for much of the expansion of the sanctuary finding here the perfect place for their more reflective way of life and they are still in residence today.

Tour

Arriving in the car park the sanctuary is concealed as it is hidden down in a hollow but when you first catch sight of it, it is a real revelation nestling against the side of Monte Egidio. Descend the path and you come to the door which leads into the earliest and original part of these buildings which when Francis settled here would have formed the communal section and round about the brothers would have found natural sheltered spots for them to retire to for their contemplative periods. Now, of course, it is difficult to imagine these humble beginnings as the impressive expansion of the years can easily obscure

Francis' original intentions.

This oldest section is now called the oratory but was first used as the dormitory and communal living area for the brothers, today it still radiates a very special prayerful atmosphere. Around the walls you will see evidence of the original occupation including relics of the saint. At the back of the oratory behind the altar is a very small entrance on the right up a few steps into a tiny chamber which was Francis' cell and like those in other sanctuaries is no advert for luxury and for us it is almost impossible to imagine sleeping here especially as this was Francis' preference.

Access to other parts of the monastery is limited as not only is Le Celle still a living community but it is also often a home to other religious and groups on retreat and therefore signs restricting entry should be respected. If you are able to it is possible to see the cells that were first added by Elias and Bonaventure and then during the Capuchin resurgence as well as the church with its lovely altar piece.

Practical Information

Le Celle is open for visits every day during daylight hours and on Sunday there is mass at 10.30am in the oratory as well as 6.30pm on Wednesday.

CORTONA

Cortona is a very ancient city with its origins firmly founded in the Etruscan period to which the melon shaped tombs on the outskirts attest. Once you have ascended to the city and parked there is one main shop- and café-lined street which leads up to the heart of this small city. Piazza della Republica is a very cosy square surrounded by imposing medieval buildings including the Palazzo Communale and just behind, in another palace, you find the Museo Civico which as well as having an eclectic collection of Etruscan finds and souvenirs of a Cortona citizen, also contains works of art by one of Cortona's most famous sons, the artist Luca Signorelli.

Signs will then direct you to the eleventh-century cathedral and the outstanding Museo Diocesano which although small contains some superb home-grown masterpieces such as the *Deposition* by Signorelli as well as great pieces by Fra Angelico and Pietro Lorenzetti.

Cortona has not only preserved its great pieces of medieval architecture but in streets like Via Ianelli you can see ordinary medieval thoroughfares with their overhanging houses still quite intact. If you can cope with the rather steep approach the Church of San Francesco is worth a visit being the second church to be dedicated to St Francis after the basilica in Assisi. Elias the controversial Minister General who became an adopted son of Cortona founded the church and is buried inside along with the artist, Signorelli. Another of Cortona's famous citizens, the artist Pietro Berrettini (better known as Pietro da Cortona), is also present here in his fresco of the Annunciation. Brother Elias gave more to Cortona than just the church as he brought back what he claimed was a relic of the true cross, which is now displayed on the high altar in an ivory reliquary.

Sanctuary of St Margherita of Cortona

High above the city stands a monument to another revered citizen of Cortona, who was also a member of the Franciscan family. Margherita did not have a conventional saintly start to her life as she soon left her home to live with a man whom she never married and had a child by him. After his death she was rejected by her family but given shelter by the Friars Minor in Cortona and from then on her devotion to St Francis grew and she was received into the Third Order dedicating the rest of her short life to serving the sick and poor. The oratory that she restored in the 1290s was built into the present building in the mid-nineteenth century by the people of Cortona, grateful for not having been affected by an epidemic of cholera. The Cortona inhabitants again showed their thanks to their patron after the Second World War when in 1947 they built the Via Crucis leading up to the shrine because the damage inflicted on many other central Italian towns had passed them

Way to the Sanctuary of St Margherita, Cortona

by. The body of St Margherita, preserved in a silver casket, today occupies pride of place in the church watching over the city below.

Practical Information
To reach the Sanctuary of St Margherita you can either take the Via Crucis from behind the Church of San Niccolo or the road from the Piazzale Garibaldi where the car park and bus stops are.
The Museo Civico is open 9.00am–1.00pm and 3.00pm–5.00pm October–March; 10.00am–7.00pm April–September. Closed on Monday. Entrance fee payable The Museo Diocesano is open 10.00am–1.00pm and 3.00pm–5.00pm November–March. During October hours are 10.00am–1.00pm and 3.30pm–6.00pm and from April–September 9.00am–1.00pm and 4.00pm–6.30pm

Lake Trasimeno

Travelling north from Perugia Lake Trasimeno can take you by surprise, as you are suddenly confronted by a large stretch of water that seems hardly ever mentioned but it is in fact the fourth largest lake in Italy after the Northern Lakes of Garda, Maggiore and Como and it was by these shores that Hannibal defeated the Romans in 217 BC. Although Trasimeno does not match the natural setting of those northern lakes it is, however, quite pretty and peaceful and can be quite easily combined with a visit to Perugia for a day's excursion from Assisi.

Access

You can reach the town of Passignano from Assisi by train or by bus via Perugia, by road it takes approximately an hour. From Passignano there are regular ferries to Isola Maggiore April–October and a skeleton service during the winter, the crossing time is about 20 minutes.

Background

Francis would have known Trasimeno well, passing it on his way to markets with his father and it is no surprise that when he wished to cut himself off completely from the world in 1211 to experience a period of utter isolation he chose the island of Isola Maggiore on Lake Trasimeno. After having gone through what must have been a challenging two years promoting the gospel throughout Italy and organizing his ever-growing band of brothers Francis must have felt pulled towards a time of reflection and recollection, to just sit back and

listen to what he felt God was instructing him to do. Doubtless he would have needed little encouragement to follow Christ's own example of retiring into the desert for forty days and so for Lent 1211 he was rowed over to the uninhabited island of Isola Maggiore to spend this time of penance in preparation for Easter.

Of course stories are recounted of miracles attached to this period in Francis' life – his having only consumed half a loaf of bread during the whole of the forty-day period, or of the fish that he had been given by a fisherman but released into the lake and which then followed him to the island out of gratitude. True or not these tales do not detract from the essence of this episode, that Francis' life was dependent upon an ever-increasing realization of God in him and in his life. Coming to Isola Maggiore can allow you a short time of reflection and relaxation away from the worries and distractions of everyday life.

Tour

Crossing over from Passignano to Isola Maggiore you soon begin to experience a sense of calm and travelling into another world. Although the island still has about one hundred inhabitants, no cars are allowed so there is little to disturb the atmosphere of peace that greets you as you disembark. From the ferry point you will find yourself in the main street, with its few houses, cafés and church, reminiscent maybe of the Venetian islands. It does not matter which way you to choose to go around the island as being only 2 km in circumference after a leisurely walk you will have reached the other side of the island where Francis spent his Lent of 1211.

If you turn left as you meet the main street you will pass the medieval Church of Bon Gesu, the House of the Captain of the People and up to your left the recently restored twelfth-century Church of San Salvatore. Continue round the lake keeping to the path which follows the shoreline and enjoy the views especially if it is a clear day and eventually you will come to a small stone structure and a statue of Francis. Near this is the Cappella dello Sbarco which marks the place where tradition has it that Francis landed on the island and nearby is a spring which sprang up after Francis

had spent time in prayer. A modern statue by the sculptor Zanetti was placed here by the Franciscan community of the Church of Santa Croce in Florence.

Just inland and slightly uphill is the small chapel which was built over the place where Francis put up a shelter of branches to serve as his 'home' on the island.

Completing the circuit of the island will take you past the ruins of the Villa Guglielmi built in the nineteenth century around what remained of the fourteenth-century Franciscan church and convent. Elena Guglielmi, whose husband presented her with the villa is known for having introduced lace-making to the island, a craft which you can see still being practised today. Taking a detour on the way back you can climb up to the Church of St Michael Archangel which is decorated with medieval frescoes.

For an appropriate meditation to use on the island, Francis' version of the Divine Praises, which he wrote while at La Verna after receiving the stigmata, could not be bettered. These devotions surely sum up how he may have felt towards God after his contemplation in this wonderful setting.

You are holy, Lord,
the only God,
and your deeds are wonderful.
You are strong, you are great,
You are the Most High,

You are the almighty King.
You, holy Father, are King of
  heaven and earth.
You are three and one,
God above all gods.
You are good, all good,
  supreme good,
Lord God, living and true.
You are love, you are wisdom,
You are humility, you are
  endurance,
You are beauty, you are
  gentleness,
You are security, you are rest,
You are joy.
You are our hope and
  happiness,
You are justice and
  moderation,
You are all our riches,
You are beauty, you are
  gentleness,
You are our protector,
You are our guardian and
  defender.
You are strength, you are
  consolation,

You are our hope, you are our
  faith,
You are our love,
You are all our sweetness,
You are our eternal life,
Great and admirable Lord,
God almighty, merciful
  Saviour.

Practical Information

Ferries operate from Passignano
to Isola Maggiore every hour
(apart from lunchtime) April–
October. Outside these months
there is a much-reduced service.
Churches on the island are open
in the morning and evening but
St Michael the Archangel may
require obtaining the key from
the custodian.
To visit the Villa Guglielmi you
need to ask permission from the
custodian.
There are a few cafés, a
restaurant and one or two
souvenir shops in the village
centre. For toilets go to one of
the cafés.

Sanctuary of Monteluco and Spoleto

An easy journey away from Assisi is the stunning medieval city of Spoleto and once again following the trail of St Francis leads us to discover another of Italy's jewels. Spoleto was a very powerful centre during the Middle Ages and therefore it is no surprise that this town has a particular mention in the accounts of Francis' life, nor that a hermitage was founded by Francis on the spectacular slopes of Monteluco which overlook the city.

Access

Spoleto can easily be reached by main road in about an hour and is equally accessible by train from Assisi (1–1½ hours depending on if it's a direct train or if you need to change at Foligno), but you will need to get the local bus to the centre as the station is a little far out.

The sanctuary of Monteluco is situated 7 km uphill from Spoleto and can be reached by road, a public bus leaves from the Piazza della Liberta in the town centre.

Background

After returning from the war with Perugia, Francis was at a loss as to how to continue his life. It seems he had lost some of his enthusiasm for following in his father's footsteps into the cloth trade and instead his imagination was caught by a more ambitious and romantic project. He engaged himself as a squire in the service of a knight from Assisi who was going to southern Italy to join the forces of Walter de Brienne in his fight against the forces of the German emperor. However, Francis did not get very far as he fell ill when the party reached Spoleto, perhaps as a result of his imprisonment in Perugia, and while asleep he had a dream which he interpreted as a clear sign of his future path. The voice in his dream asked him bluntly where he was going, and when Francis answered, asked him whether it was better to serve the servant or the master. Francis as always accepts the command he receives from the Lord – to go back to Assisi to wait for the call to a different type of fight involving other forms of weaponry and rewards.

Spoleto was an obvious place for the brothers to come to as part of their evangelizing mission and tradition has them settling near the ancient chapel of St Elias which is now within the Rocca fortress, but there is no doubt that they went up the mountain to find their oasis of peace and tranquillity. The slopes of Monteluco must have been well known to Francis, and as it was also known as a place of hermitage from early times, it was the ideal place for another centre to which the brothers could retire to concentrate on prayer. The sanctuary dates from the year 1218.

Sanctuary of Monteluco

Monteluco is known not only for the sanctuary but also because it is situated 800 metres high in woods as a summer mountain resort providing a cool and quiet haven during the unrelentingly hot months of July and August which is the reason for passing several attractive hotels on the way up. The name Monteluco is an ancient one and the meaning, which is patently accurate, is 'sacred mountain.'

Monteluco did not suffer expansion like the other sanctuaries and so remains very much the picture of peace and isolation; and just as Francis would have been, we are struck more by the glorious natural surroundings than the imposing buildings. What to visit is immediately obvious: start first with the church on your right, which was built over Francis' cell and oratory and which you can still see, and again be impressed by the uncompromising way in which Francis although utterly human could comply with and even delight in according with the

demands of a poor life. After the church go through the cloister where you can see the cells inhabited by friars up until quite recently.

All around this central area the brothers would have found their own space which would act as their particular grotto and there was no more famous occupant after Francis than St Anthony of Padua, whose grotto can be seen nearby. Don't confuse the church in the quadrangle with the small chapel just outside it which almost certainly predates Francis and is dedicated to St Catherine.

Spoleto

Spoleto has much to recommend it and a single visit hardly does it justice, but below are a few suggestions for what you could fit into a day along with a visit to Monteluco. A guide book is recommended for more detailed descriptions.

If you have arrived in Spoleto by road you cannot have failed to notice the spectacular viaduct which connects Spoleto with the slopes of Monteluco, this is the Ponte delle Torri, designed by Gattapone and constructed in the mid-fourteenth century. At 230 metres long and 80 metres high it is one of the largest in Italy and a masterpiece of engineering. It is a good idea if you are arriving by private coach to start here and have the coach meet you at the car park below the city for your return journey, thus avoiding any unecessary uphill climbing! Walking across the bridge is quite an experience, and it offers a unique view of the city, especially as access is for pedestrians only. That the bridge meets the Rocca fortress is no coincidence, because they were both built at the command of the same man, Cardinal Albornoz who acted as the pope's representative during the Avignon schism and through him the papacy reasserted its claims over various territories. Fortress and bridge together were to ensure that the pope's man in Spoleto could never be unseated because of a siege – they provided a supply line or escape route as required. Lucrezia Borgia was for a short time resident in the fortress when she and her second husband governed the city and its solid and impenetrable character meant that it served as a prison to as recently as 1983, but will soon have a less controversial role in housing Spoleto's art gallery.

Descending into the city you will soon see to your right the duomo (cathedral) which is one of the finest examples of Romanesque architecture in the region. Crossing the lovely wide open piazza (which is used as an open air stage during the Festival of Two Worlds each year in June) in front of the cathedral you have time to consider the unusual façade, with the Renaissance portico

and above it eight rose windows around a mosaic by Solsternus. Inside, the church changes its style to Baroque owing to renovations in the seventeenth century, although parts of the polychrome pavement are still original and the apse proudly shows off the Life of the Virgin frescoes by the fifteenth-century master, Fra Filippo Lippi. Behind the altar the right-hand chapel is dedicated to Spoleto's prized possession of an icon of the Madonna which tradition has it Frederick Barbarossa brought back from Constantinople and donated to the city. Before you leave the cathedral make sure you do not miss the Chapel of Reliquaries in the north aisle because preserved there is the only example, besides that in the Basilica of St Francis in Assisi, of Francis' handwriting (it is a letter written to Brother Leo).

Continuing downhill by way of the Via Saffi you pass the archbishop's palace through which you gain entrance to the Diocesan Museum and the now redundant church of Sant'Eufemia. A visit here is well worth while, for not only is this an exquisite Romanesque church but one of the few in which the *matronium* (upper gallery for women attending church services) is preserved in tact.

Taking a left fork after the archbishop's palace will lead you to the pretty Piazza Mercato where a small market is still held, and from there you can start to discover the impressive Roman inheritance of this city with the Arco di Druso, dedicated in AD 23 to Drusus and Germanicus, and below which you can see remains of shops and a temple from the same period. Continue through the medieval town with its very appealing shops with their old-fashioned shop fronts and you cross over the Piazza della Liberta to reach the Archaeological Museum which includes the remains of the Roman theatre.

Practical Information
Sanctuary of Monteluco Open daily 9am–12.00 and 3.00–6.00pm
Duomo (Cathedral) Open 7.30am–12.30pm; 3.00–5.30pm (6.30pm March–September)
Museo Diocesano and Sant'Eufemia Open daily 10.30am–12.30pm; 3.30–7.00pm. Entrance fee payable
Archaeological Museum Open daily 9.00am–1.30pm; 2.30–7.00pm. Entrance fee payable

11. Archway leading to San Francesco Piccolo

12. One of Assisi's old gateways, Porta San Giacomo

13. Assisi is full of steps!

14. Traditional Assisi embroidery in the making

15. Santa Maria degli Angeli

16. Poggio Bustone

17. Le Celle

18. Entrance to the Sanctuary of Fonte Colombo

19. Statue of St Francis marking where he disembarked on Isola Maggiore

Perugia

Perugia sprawls across the top of a hill dominating the plains below, today as it has for centuries. The capital of the region of Umbria and an important commercial centre it has a history and a grandeur to complement its title, and provides a fascinating day out whether you are looking for art, architecture or archaeology or just a pleasant excursion in an elegant, but very beautiful, Italian city.

Access

Perugia is easily reached from Assisi by public bus. There is a regular service which leaves from the centre of Assisi and takes about an hour, but by private coach should only take about forty minutes.

Background

A brief look at Perugia will very quickly reveal evidence of a distinguished past spanning more than two and a half millennia – from being one of the twelve cities of the Etruscan Confederation to its position today as the regional administrative centre. During the medieval period Perugia, although an independent commune, frequently affiliated itself to the papacy, thus adding to the reasons why Assisi would feel threatened by its powerful neighbour and for the disputes which arose between the two towns. For Francis this antagonism proved to be the springboard for recognizing his vocation for after a brief, but disastrous, battle between the two he found himself a prisoner of war in Perugia. The battle took place in the plain below

the city at a spot called Collestrada, near which there is now a very modern shopping centre! Perugia grew in strength and importance during the Middle Ages and this is reflected in the impressive communal buildings in the centre of the city which are some of the finest in Italy.

Perugia's golden age gave way to an era marked by disputes between the leading families which were finally brought to an end by the imposition of papal control which lasted into the nineteenth century. Part of the new Italian nation after 1860, Perugia benefited from industrial developments and began to expand rapidly, so that it is now one of the leading commercial and financial centres of this region, even having its own premier league football team. One of the positive results of Perugia's modernization was the founding of the Perugina chocolate factory, which boasts among its products the famous Bacci (kisses) and the town celebrates this claim to fame every year in October with a chocolate festival.

Perugia

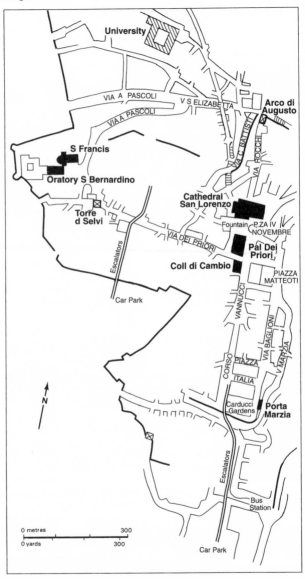

Plan of Perugia

Tour of major sights

Suggesting an itinerary for a brief visit to Perugia is paved with difficulties because there is just too much to see and including something means doing so at the expense of another equally deserving place. Perugia's overall image has sometimes been described in guidebooks as 'staid' or 'interesting' rather than 'fascinating' thus giving the impression that a single trip here would suffice, but this does the city no justice. To really see the city would take a good few days of exploration by foot but because of the normal restrictions on one's time what is attempted below is an itinerary which would help you profit from a half or full day's visit.

The starting point for the tour is the series of escalators which take you up into the old city from near the bus station, which is also where private coaches can set down passengers. This ascent into the city is probably one of the most unusual in Europe as not only do you climb 50 metres, but you pass through a buried city. When Pope Paul III asserted his authority over Perugia in the sixteenth century it meant having to crush certain powerful families and a sure sign that he had achieved this was by constructing his own place on top of their houses. However, the architect, Sangallo obviously felt some regret over having to do so and saved the series of streets which you see as you reach the top of the escalators.

Corso Vannucci

From the escalator exit the first turn to your left and you find yourself in the Carducci Gardens (named after a famous nineteenth-century Italian poet), and from here on a clear day you have a wonderful view of the Umbrian Valley including Assisi. After the gardens go back into the main square and cross over to the pedestrianized main thoroughfare of Perugia which is called Corso Vannucci after the real name of the famous painter known as Perugino after the city where he made his fame as an artist. You can see the work of Perugino at its best in the Collegio di Cambio which is on the left of the street as you go up it and forms part of the complex of public buildings built for the city in the thirteenth century and used by the bankers' guild to ajudicate financial disputes.

The Palazzo dei Priori which is the name applied to the whole of this row of buildings (which the Collegio di Cambio is part of) and which stretches right up to the main square, is one of the most impressive shows of the power of the medieval commune anywhere in Italy. The 'priors' referred to in this sense are not religious figures but magistrates of the commune and their 'offices' were built at the end of the thirteenth century and still today house the city's administration, while at the same time being home to the National Gallery of Umbria on the third floor. The gallery should be seen if you have time as it has among its collection some of the finest works of the early Renaissance including paintings by Piero della Francesca and Perugino and wonderful sculpture by Arnolfo di Cambio.

Before you start to explore the square move round to the side of the Palazzo dei Priori and climb the stairs to the Sala dei Notari for a display of real civic pride, still used today for the good of the city to host lectures, concerts and exhibitions. Around the walls are displayed the coats of arms of the *Podestas* (mayors) of Perugia but more interestingly, though more difficult to see are the late thirteenth-century frescoes in the ceiling depicting scenes from the Old Testament, probably the work of a student of the Roman artist, Piero Cavallini.

Piazza IV Novembre

At first sight the main piazza of the city is something of an anti-climax after the grandeur of the buildings of the Palazzo dei Priori but a little time spent looking around you reveals a delightful view of the centre, in no way symmetrical or all of one period, in short a snapshot of Perugia's tremendous historical and cultural inheritance. Standing with your

back to the Sala dei Notari you are facing the Fontana Maggiore, one of the greatest masterpieces of Italian medieval sculpture, although it was constructed for a purely practical reason – that of guaranteeing a water supply in any situation and thereby ensuring Perugia's independence. Fra Bevignate designed a series of aqueducts to transport water a distance of 5km outside the city and to cap this engineering feat the celebrated father and son Nicola and Giovanni Pisano, famed for their work in Pisa Cathedral, were commissioned to construct a fitting fountain. After several years of renovation the Fontana Maggiore was uncovered in 1999 and can now be seen in all its glory and it does need some careful looking at as the detail is breathtaking. There are two levels of sculpted panels, the lower one reveals the months of the year accompanied by their zodiac signs and also reliefs representing the liberal arts and scenes from the Old Testament and two of Aesop's fables. On the upper section twenty-four panels show figures from Perugia's history, the Old and New Testaments and personifications of towns associated with Perugia.

Now walk beyond the fountain to the Cathedral of San Lorenzo (one of the patron saints of the city) but take a brief look at the outside before going in and believe your first

The Fontana Maggiore and Cathedral in Piazza IV Novembre.

impression that it is unfinished, though in spite of that it is still an impressive Romanesque church. Don't miss the pulpit attached to the exterior wall at quite a height, this was put there by the city for the great Franciscan preacher, Bernardine of Siena, who addressed the citizens of Perugia on many occasions on the subject of their unChristian behaviour. In particular Bernardine railed against the materialism of society at the time and as a result he invited people to rid themselves of the possessions which would prevent their spiritual development, burning these things (including women's hairpieces) in the piazza in a ceremony known as the 'bonfire of the vanities'.

Take the side door into the cathdral and stand still for a few moments while you adapt to the darkness inside and gradually come to appreciate the very high, spacious and elegant interior which contrasts starkly with the clumsy exterior. This uncluttered arrangement encourages you to walk around and investigate the church and its works of art but entering from the side door your attention is drawn to a small altar standing in the middle of the nave which displays an image of Madonna delle Grazie, much venerated by the Perugians.

Another prize of Perugia is kept well hidden in the chapel to the right of the main entrance as you look towards it with your back to the high altar, this is the relic of the 'wedding ring of Our Lady'. However to see it you will have to time your visit for 29 or 30 July, which is the only time during the year it is displayed!

Off the beaten track – medieval streets and Roman arches

If your appetite has been whetted enough and you have the time and energy to discover more of this fascinating city, then you can follow a simple circular route which will take you back in time more than two thousand years.

From the Piazza IV Novembre go along the side of the Palazzo dei Priori and veer left to join the Via dei Priori which will reveal the heart of medieval Perugia with typical tall houses of this period lining the steeply descending street and it was in this area that the artist Perugino probably lived. As you go down this continually changing thoroughfare you can, if you are very observant, count six churches although you will probably only find two or three open, but they are well worth a look inside and testify to the vital part they played in medieval society.

About halfway down the Via dei Priori on your left you will come to the Torre degli Sciri, over 46 metres high and the only domestic tower surviving from the Middle Ages and as such it rather stands out as an oddity. However there were

once as many as five hundred towers like this in Perugia, their purpose was twofold: First, to provide a safe place to stay in case of attack, and second a sign of 'keeping up with the Jones's' – if your neighbour has one you have to have one too!

The narrow built-up street at the end opens up quite suddenly and you are faced by an open space that in the Middle Ages was a meadow area outside the city walls and here side by side are two churches dedicated to St Francis and St Bernardine of Siena respectively. To the left facing you across the road is the Oratory of St Bernardine a jewel of Renaissance art and architecture, built in honour of the saint after his canonization in 1450 and financed by the citizens of Perugia. Subtly constructed in polychrome marble, the façade looks its best in the early evening of a fine day when the setting sun shows off the delicate pink and blue coloured stone. St Bernardine features in the lunette and below the sculptor Duccio worked in scenes depicting miracles performed by the saint. Inside the church your gaze is drawn towards the rather unusual altar which is in fact an early fourth-century sarcophagus which was recycled to be used as the tomb of Francis' companion, Beato (Blessed) Egidio.

Next to the oratory is the large and imposing thirteenth-century church of St Francis which unfortunately is permanently closed because of subsidence. As you continue down the Via Pascoli you pass through an area which was the quarter occupied by craftsmen but now home to the modern university (the ancient former home of Perugia University can be seen in Piazza Matteotti which can be reached from Corso Vannucci). At the junction with Via S. Elisabetta turn right up the hill and after passing under an arch on top of which once ran the aqueduct that leads to the Fontana Maggiore, climb the flight of stairs at the end and then turn back on yourself to see the impressive Arco Etrusco (Arco d'Augusto) which, as the dual name suggests, has a complicated history. Begun in the third century BC during the Etruscan era the Roman emperor made sure that the arch paid homage to him after he had conquered the city, and therefore on the upper part of the arch one can see the inscription 'Augusta Perusia' (Augustus' Perugia). However, this was not the last alteration, that the arch saw as 1,500 years later a loggia was added to the trapezoidal tower to finish it off.

Climbing is in order once again as you return to Piazza IV Novembre via the ancient street of Via Ulisse Rocchi, where near the top in the Enoteca on the right you can see and even taste an extensive range of regional wines.

Depending on your stamina and timetable you can stop here or return to the escalators by a different route turning left off the Corso Vannucci into the lovely Piazza Matteotti, a long rectangular square built on Etruscan foundations and flanked by elegant medieval palaces which once housed the university and the house of the Captain of the People. Through the arch on the left-hand side you can reach the two-storeyed market, which besides offering a wide choice of local produce and other goods, is also another great vantage point for taking in the view of the whole valley. To return back to the Carducci Gardens take the left-hand road from the top of the piazza, Via Baglioni, but the energetic can divert down the Via Marzia to see another remaining Etruscan gateway, the Porta Marzia.

There are many other fascinating churches and historical sites to be seen in and around Perugia such as San Domenico and the Archaeological Museum, Sant'Angelo and San Pietro but to visit these would demand much more time and also stamina as they are situated on the outskirts of the old city. Just outside the city are Etruscan tombs (the Ipogei dei Volumni) that can be visited if you have access to private transport.

Opening Times
Collegio del Cambio Open 9.00am–12.30pm; 2.30pm–5.30pm. November to

Perugia

February closes at 2.00pm and not open on Mondays. Entrance fee payable

National Gallery of Umbria Open 9.00am–7.00pm. Closed first Monday of every month. Entrance fee payable

Sala dei Notari Open 9.00am–1.00pm; 3.00pm–7.00pm. Closed Mondays except peak season

Cathedral of San Lorenzo Closed from 12.00pm–4.00pm

Easy Excursions from Assisi

It is easy to come to Assisi to visit the obvious places associated with St Francis and then look further afield to 'bigger fish' such as Florence or Rome for other excursions, and while these are quite possible it is a shame that the majority of visitors and pilgrims miss out on the lovely countryside and fascinating towns that lie within a short drive from Assisi. Also, to discover these lands is to know a little more of the country that Francis was familiar with. Seeing that this landscape can help us understand better Francis' relationship with nature and perhaps we can learn to see like him that God is really present in all living things.

Below is a proposed itinerary that could fill half a day or easily all day depending on the time spent in each place.

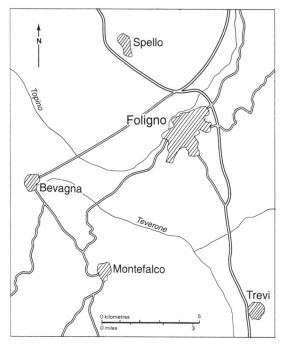

Location of Bevagna

Access

Although there is a bus service that runs from Foligno to Bevagna and Montefalco, there is limited frequency and therefore private transport is really necessary for this excursion. However, it is quite easy to reach Spello from Assisi either by bus or train.

PIAN D'ARCA

Below Monte Subasio, the vast valley of Umbria stretches out in all directions and presents a great contrast to the mountainous situation of Assisi. It is down in this plain that a small monument records Francis' famous sermon to the birds at an isolated place called Pian d'Arca. The preaching to the birds is mentioned in several of the early biographies including the *Life of St Francis* written by Thomas of Celano and the *Little Flowers*. Whether there was in fact one specific incident and whether or not it occurred at this place is not really relevant as the imagery of these accounts seems entirely appropriate in this quiet and pretty spot. Francis is said to have reminded the birds that they had a duty to praise God their creator, as he had clothed them with feathers and given them wings to fly, and then after blessing them soundly commanded them to fly to all corners of the earth to proclaim the greatness of God.

BEVAGNA

Bevagna is a charming, ancient town which also has the reputation for being very friendly and has preserved its Umbrian character without becoming spoilt by tourism. Bevagna was in its early days a relatively important Roman town as the Via Flaminia ran right through it, but when this was diverted around Spoleto Mevania (as it was known) became the quiet backwater it still is today. The medieval traditions of the town are celebrated in a unique festival at the beginning of June called the Mercato delle Gaite where artisans reproduce ancient crafts in the town centre.

Whether you arrive from the main car park or enter at the higher end of the town through the Porta Cannara, you will notice the walls still quite in tact. At the upper end you cannot fail to see evidence of the Roman past of the town in the Piazza Garibaldi where there is a church that was once a Roman temple, obvious by the use of typical flat red bricks in its construction. Just nearby in the Via Porta Guelfa a wonderful mosaic dating from second century AD, features octopus, lobsters and dolphins. Just north of here near the Porta Foligno you can see traces of the Roman amphitheatre in the pattern formed by the present-day houses.

All roads eventually filter into the main street Corso Matteotti, which follows the line of the old Via Flaminia and makes an ideal route for 'passegiata' with its typical shops, several

Church of San Michele Archangelo in Piazza Silvestri

interesting little churches and inviting cafés. Corso Matteotti leads into one of the loveliest town squares in Umbria, Piazza Filippo Silvestri, where one can easily spend an hour or so and it should not be rushed through. On the left is the handsome gothic Palazzo dei Consoli, which was the seat of local government until the nineteenth century, but which is still used for exhibitions and to house the Tourist Information Office. However, the real surprise of this building is discovered by climbing the exterior staircase at the side and you find yourself in the beautifully restored Teatro Torto which is 130 years old and still in use as a theatre.

The unique character of this complex continues when you step into the Church of San Silvestro, which although severe and simple in style is a masterpiece of Romanesque architecture with a lovely barrel vaulted nave and elegant columns capped with Corinthian capitals.

Opposite San Silvestro is San Michele Archangelo, the parish church of Bevagna dating from the end of the twelfth century and of great interest but at present closed for extensive restoration, in part as a result of the earthquakes of 1997–98.

MONTEFALCO

About 6 km from Bevagna lies the small medieval town of Montefalco, but quite in contrast as whereas Bevagna lies almost on the flat, Montefalco is at a height of some 500 metres giving it its particular advantage of being able to see for some distance across the valley. For this reason Montefalco is called the 'Ringhiera d'Umbra', (balcony of Umbria) and from various vantage points around the town it is possible to see right across to Assisi and Perugia in one direction and Foligno in the other. Montefalco probably gained its present name from occupation of the town by Emperor Frederick Barbarossa in the thirteenth century, whose arms included an eagle (falco). Montefalco is a good example of the extent to which Francis influenced medieval urban society, as in this small place there is not one but three churches which have a Franciscan connection: the church of St Francis, the monastery of San Fortunato just outside the town and the Convent of Santa Chiara founded by Chiara of Montefalco who had belonged to the Franciscan Third Order before becoming an Augustinian nun.

From the main car park walk up to the town walls and enter through the Porta Sant'Agostino and then follow the main street, Corso G. Mameli through to the Piazza del Comune, a very pretty open main square with the Palazzo del Comune and its typical tower. In the piazza you will find a good *enoteca* (wine shop) which sells local wines including the famous Sagrantino, which is a very heavy red wine of at least 13% alcohol and can only be found in this area. On the way from Bevagna to Montefalco you can see the vineyards where the sagrantino grapes and other local types are grown. If you prefer a tasting the bar/restaurant on the corner can provide this as well as other typical products of the area.

Montefalco's great claim to fame apart from its wine and views lies in the Church of San Francesco, which is now a museum and can be reached from the Via Ringhiera d'Umbra that leads off the Piazza del Comune. The Church of San Francesco, dating from the 1330s, ceased being used as such in the nineteenth century and is now owned by the town and forms part of the Museo Civico. Reminding worshippers of the merits of the patron saint of a particular church was one of the principal functions of the decoration and to this end the painter Benozzo Gozzoli, known at the time for his collaboration with Fra Angelico in Orvieto cathedral, was commissioned by the Franciscans in 1450 to make a fitting tribute to their founder. *The Life of St Francis* has centre stage in the main apse of the nave, and is considered to be Gozzoli's finest work serving as a role model for Umbrian painting in the succeeding fifty years.

To find a fantastic panoramic view of the surrounding countryside either continue down to the end of the Via Ringhiera d'Umbra or as you go back along the main street take a right-hand turn.

SPELLO

Overshadowed by Assisi at the other end of Mount Subasio, Spello is often neglected but unfortunately so for Spello is not only very pretty but also rich in Roman and medieval sites. The town is also known for the *infiorita*, the spectacular celebration of Corpus Christi every year on the Sunday after the feast day, when carpets of flowers are laid in the streets for the passage of a great procession. Spello, like Assisi, looks at its best in the early evening because of the glow of the pinkish local stone in the late sunlight.

A short visit to the town should take in the Porta Venere, the best preserved of Spello's Roman gateways and one of the finest in Italy with its twelve-sided towers flanking the three arches. The name Spello is derived from the Roman Hispellum and it was at one

time an important staging post on the Via Flaminia.

Not too far, but up a fairly steep incline, you reach the Piazza della Repubblica and the former Palazzo Communale which in the atrium houses a collection of Roman fragments. Continue up along the Via Cavour and you come to the Church of Santa Maria Maggiore that at first glance might seem like a rather ordinary medieval church with a Baroque facelift, but the trip inside is well worth it. The interior decoration would be quite satisfying enough but the Baglioni Chapel on your left as you walk up to the nave is more than adequate compensation for the effort of the climb to get here. This chapel like so many in many medieval churches was for the private use of a wealthy family who had the means to employ a well-known artist to put the icing on the cake. Pinturicchio (not his real name but given this title because of the rich colours he used) was called here to carry out this work in 1500 and it is considered to be one of his finest for its delicate and detailed treatment of the three scenes of the Annunciation, the adoration of the shepherds and Christ among the priests in the temple. Whatever you do, do not forget your loose change to pay to light up the mural or you will miss the exquisite detail of the landscape in the background and even a self-portrait of Pinturicchio himself below in the Annuciation scene.

Do not leave the chapel without first noticing the flooring made from original sixteenth-century majolica tiles from nearby Deruta.

Opening Times
Bevagna
Roman Mosaic and Teatro Torti Open on request from the Tourist Information Office. Churches Open during the morning and afternoon but closed for normal Italian lunchtime approximately from midday until 3 or 4pm

Montefalco
Museum of San Francesco Open 10.30am–1.00pm; 2.30–5.00pm (later in summmer). Closed on Mondays November–February. Churches See notes above for Bevagna

Spello
Church of Santa Maria Maggiore Open morning and afternoon but closed at lunchtime 12.30–2.30pm

Excursions Further Afield

It is very tempting when visiting Italy not to want to miss any of the highlights that we see frequently represented in travel articles and programmes in the media, and prior to coming to Assisi and Umbria it is easy to have great plans. However, as this little guidebook shows, for followers of Francis, pilgrim and tourist alike, this area is a real box of delights and once there the temptation to go very far will undoubtedly diminish. Given the bias of this travelogue there is not the space here to deal with the great centres of Rome, Florence and Siena sufficiently – another guidebook will be necessary!

Rome, Florence and Siena are reachable from Assisi but please note the remarks below regarding timing and distance because all of these three choices really demand a full day's excursion, leaving early and returning reasonably late. The weather can also influence what one can manage in a day and it is worth bearing this in mind when organizing an itinerary, especially if the tour is planned for the summer period, due to the heat.

ROME

Access

The best way to reach Rome from Assisi is by train from the station in Santa Maria degli Angeli. Fast trains only take about two hours and by leaving between 7.00am and 8.00am you would be assured of a reasonable amount of time in the city. Another advantage of travelling by rail is that the Termini station in Rome is quite central and both the bus and metro systems operate from here and can take you quickly to other parts of the heart of the city. Alternatively, a group could travel by private coach but the journey time will vary according to traffic conditions in the suburbs and there is the added problem of where the coach can drop off and pick up passengers. It is worth remembering that a standard public transport ticket can be used for both bus and metro and is valid for 75 minutes for any number of journeys during that time.

Suggested itineraries

It is very easy to try and do too much in one day, but at the end to feel that you have not seen anything properly and so it often works better to confine the day's sightseeing around a few things that you find really interesting or that are particularly relevant to your visit to Italy as a whole. Below

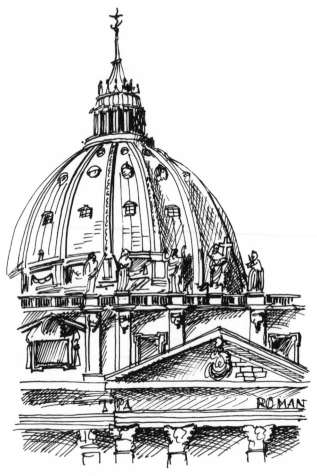

St Peter's, Rome

are two suggestions for itineraries that would suit a first-time visitor, including sites that are quite close together to facilitate an interesting but not overrushed day's touring. In both cases it has been assumed that St Peter's is an essential part of a pilgrimage programme. Visits to museums have not been included in the suggestions as these would generally be too time-consuming for a day.

Vatican and ancient roman sites

Vatican – Castel Sant'Angelo – Piazza Navona and Pantheon – Campidoglio – Forum – Colosseum

From the station you can easily take a bus or the underground to near the Vatican and allow one to two hours for viewing the colonnade and the interior with time to take the lift up to the base of the dome to enjoy the spectacular views. The tour can continue on foot or by bus although walking takes you on a spectacular route down the Via della Conciliazione past the Roman emperor Hadrian's mausoleum, Castel Sant' Angelo and across the River Tiber. Once on the other side you can choose whether to go straight to Piazza Venezia or take a detour via the beautiful Piazza Navona, once a chariot-race stadium and hence its shape and also the great Roman temple of the Pantheon. (If you happen to be in Rome in December Piazza Navona is the

place to go for Christmas decorations and gifts, as there is a large craft fair held here.)

Many people find the Victor Emmanuel Monument in Piazza Venezia rather hideous but around it lie some real jewels: Trajan's column and the square designed by Michelangelo, the Campidoglio erected near one of ancient Rome's most holiest of sites, the Temple of Jupiter. Anyone climbing the steps up to the Campidoglio is doubly rewarded by the graceful square and from the other side a wonderful view over the remains of the Roman forum.

To finish the day off if time permits it is a short distance up the Via dei Fori Imperiali to the Colosseum and from there the metro can take you back to Termini station.

Vatican and favourite roman sights

Vatican – Piazza del Popolo – Piazza Spagna and Spanish Steps – Trevi Fountain – Quirinal

Follow the above itinerary but after the Vatican take a bus or the metro (to Flaminia stop) and see one of the loveliest and Roman of all the squares in the city, Piazza del Popolo. The Church of Santa Maria del Popolo in the square, though small, contains more than its fair share of works of art with chapels decorated by Pinturicchio, Raphael and Bernini, not forgetting Caravaggio. From Piazza del Popolo it is easy to get to Piazza

Spagna and the famous Spanish Steps, but you can choose between the high road which runs beside the start of the Borghese Gardens and from where there is a magnificent view of the city, or the lower route along the Via del Babuino. Piazza Spagna is a place to just spend time. The poet Keats must have thought so as he lived in a house at the bottom of the steps.

From Piazza Spagna it is a pleasant short walk to the Trevi Fountain, into which tradition has it that you have to throw a coin over your shoulder to ensure that you will return! Returning to the station from the Trevi Fountain you can easily pass the elegant and picturesque area around the Quirinal, the presidential palace. If you still have spare time you could visit the great Basilica of Santa Maria Maggiore near the station.

FLORENCE

Access

Florence is a similar distance from Assisi as Rome is, so an early departure is in order whether travelling by road or rail. Whatever way you choose to go the journey time is about three hours. Santa Maria Novella railway station is quite central being only a ten-minute walk from the cathedral, whereas the coach park is at least twenty minutes on foot.

Suggested itinerary

Florence, like Rome, is an embarrassment of riches and a day's visit can merely provide a taster of the city's sights and for this reason the museums, however attractive they are have not been included in the programme here. If you did want to see the Uffizi, Accademia or Bargello it would be advisable to make just one or two of these the object of your visit and to make an advance booking so that precious time is not wasted standing in a queue. This itinerary is designed for the first-time visitor to take in the principal sights.

Santa Maria Novella – Cathedral – Baptistry – Orsanmichele – Piazza della Signoria (Santa Croce) – Ponte Vecchio

From the station it is just a few minutes walk to one of Florence's most lovely churches, Santa Maria Novella. Built by the Dominicans and refurbished in Renaissance style, there is no shortage of work by masters such as Filippo Lippi and Ghirlandaio. Cross the square and walk up to the Duomo di Santa Maria del Fiore (the cathedral) remarkable for Brunelleschi's dome, the bell tower designed by Giotto and the Baptistry of St John noted for the bronze doors and interior mosaics. Take the main shopping street, Via dei Calzaiuoli opposite the baptistry and en route you pass the most original church of Orsanmichele which owes its

Cathedral of Santa Maria del Fiore, Florence

rich decoration outside and in to the powerful Florentine medieval guilds, the Arti.

The Via dei Calzaiuoli ends up in one of Florence's most photographed spots, Piazza della Signoria, still the seat of local government overlooked by the giant watchtower. Off one corner you can see the government offices established by Cosimo de Medici and now better known as the Uffizi art gallery. Depending on time you could now visit the great Franciscan church of Santa Croce. (NB It does not reopen until 3.00pm after closing at 12.30pm). Giotto, who had worked so famously in Assisi, was also commissioned here to paint scenes of the life of St Francis. No visit to Florence would be complete without that view from the Ponte Vecchio,

the only medieval bridge to survive the Second World War, still sporting goldsmiths' and jewellers' shops as it has done for centuries.

SIENA

Access

It is not easy to reach Siena by public transport as it involves two changes by train and the station is some way from the centre, which would mean having to leave very shortly after arriving! On the other hand being not so far away from Assisi as Florence it should take only about two hours by road and the public car park is reasonably near the city centre. One word of warning, Siena is built on hills and no matter which way you go from one sight to another it will involve going up inclines, but at least strict traffic restrictions apply excluding the majority of cars from the historic centre.

Suggested itinerary

Siena obviously is of significant interest for the pilgrim and tourist alike and there is much to discover with too little time in one day to do so but below is a 'taster' of the main highlights of Siena.

San Domenico – House of St Catherine of Siena – Cathedral – Il Campo – Palazzo Pubblico

From the car park cross the road and you will come quickly to the Church of San Domenico, a great barn of a place and typical in design of churches run by the Dominican order for whom preaching was a major part of their mission. Inside the austerity and bareness is offset by the lovely stained glass behind the main altar. Siena's great patron saint is the mystic, St Catherine (1347–80), who became a Dominican tertiary and spent much of her time in this church. A rather gruesome reminder of this is the chapel on the right where her head is preserved in a marble tabernacle!

Descending from San Domenico you soon come to the House of St Catherine, where the saint lived for most of her life, some of it in total seclusion. Uphill and into the heart of the old city you cannot miss the cathedral with its striped stone façade, which had

it not been for the Black Death would have been enlarged to almost twice its present size. The interior is as remarkable as the outside with exquisite marble inlaid flooring, a magnificent pulpit by Pisano and the glorious Piccolomini Library with frescoes by Pinturicchio.

After a sufficient break for rest and refreshment there is only one direction to head in and that is towards the main square of Siena, Il Campo, which is one of the most impressive in Italy because of its size, shell-like shape and being sited on a slope. The Campo is known throughout the world for its famous horse race the Palio which is run around the square, with representatives of the city's seventeen *contrade* (districts) taking part. The function of the main piazza in Italy is to accommodate the seat of local government and in this the Campo is no exception boasting the Palazzo Pubblico on one side, which still serves its original purpose. Evidence of Siena's once great civic pride lies in the vast chambers upstairs where the town leaders were strongly reminded of how to rule by the fourteenth-century frescoes of the Allegory of Good and Bad Government by Ambrogio Lorenzetti.

Opening Times
Rome

St Peter's Open all day from early morning to evening (unless there is a ceremony taking place.

Palazzo Pubblico in the Piazza del Campo

Papal Audiences take place on Wednesday morning if the pope is in Rome. If it is warm enough they are held in the piazza in front of St Peter's, otherwise in the audience hall.
Dome is open 8.00am–5.00pm (6.00pm in summer) fee payable
Colosseum Open Tuesday–Saturday 9.00am–6.00pm (3.00pm in winter)
Sunday 9.00am–1.00pm. Closed Mondays. Entrance fee payable
Florence
Cathedral Open Monday–Saturday 10.00am–5.00pm (except first Saturday of the month when it closes at 3.30pm); Sunday 1–5.00pm
Baptistry Open 12.00–6.30pm; Sundays 8.30am–1.30pm. Entrance fee payable
Santa Maria Novella Open 8.00am–12.00; 4–6.00pm (5.00pm Saturdays)
Orsanmichele Open 9.00am–12.00; 4–6.00pm. Closed first and last Sunday each month
Santa Croce Summer opening 8.00am–6.30pm (Sunday

Excursions Further Afield

8.00am–12.30pm; 3–6.30pm);
Winter 8.00am–12.30pm;
3–6.30pm daily
Siena
San Domenico Open
7.00am–1.00pm; 3–6.30pm
Cathedral Summer opening early
morning–7.30pm; Winter

7.30am–1.00pm; 2.30–5.00pm
St Catherine's House Open
9.00am–12.30pm; 3.30–6.00pm
Palazzo Pubblico Open
9.30am–6.30pm in summer;
10.00am–3.15pm in winter.
Admission charge

Parliamo Italiano – Let's Speak Italian!

English is only widely spoken in the main cities and tourist areas but outside here you will find that your visit will be greatly enhanced by being able to speak a few useful phrases. A phrase book can come in very handy, but for quick reference the phrases below should be of help in many practical situations. A rough phonetic guide is given but only practice will tell you if you have got it right! However, the Italians are very appreciative of any effort made in their language and it is certainly a good way of having more contact with Italians.

Greetings

Hello/Good Morning	*Buongiorno*	Bwonjorno
Hi!	*Ciao*	Chow
Good afternoon/evening	*Buona sera*	Bwona serra
Good Night	*Buona Notte*	Bwona nottay
Goodbye	*Arriverderci*	Arrivairdairchee

Basic Conversation words and phrases

Yes	*Si*	See
No	*No*	No
		'o' sound is short as in 'hot'
Do you speak English?	*Parla inglese?*	Parla inglaysay
I don't understand	*Non capisco*	Non capeesco
Excuse me (in a crowd)	*Permesso*	Pairmesso
Excuse me	*Mi scusi*	Mee Scoozee
I'm sorry	*Mi dispiace*	Mee dispiachay
I am British	*Sono inglese*	Sono inglaysay

Shopping

I would like	*Vorrei*	Vorayee
How much is it?	*Quanto costa*	Qwanto costa
I'll have this/that one	*Prendo questo/quello*	Prendo qwesto/qwello
Do you have?	*Avete*	Avaytay
Thank you	*Grazie*	Gratsiay
Please	*Per favore*	Pair favoray

Directions

Where is?	*Dov'e*	Dovay

| Is it far/near? | *E lontano/vicino* | Ay lontarno/ veecheeno |
| On the left/right | *A sinistra/destra* | A seeneestra |

Drinks and snacks

An espresso coffee	*Un caffè*	Oon caffay
A long black coffee	*Un caffè americano*	Oon caffay americano
A cappuccino coffee	*Un cappuccino*	Oon cappucheeno
A tea with milk	*Un tè con latte*	Oon tay con latay
An orange juice	*Un succo d'arancia*	Oon sooco darancha
Mineral water fizzy/ natural	*Un aqua minerale gassata/non gassata*	Oon aqwa mineralay gassata/non gassata
A beer small/medium/ large	*Una birra piccola/ media/grande*	Oona beera piccola/ maydia/granday
A white/red wine	*Un vino bianco/rosso*	oon veeno beeanco/ rosso
A cheese/ham roll	*Un panino con formaggio/ prosciutto*	Oon paneeno con fomarjo/proshooto
A cake	*Una pasta*	Oona pasta
A sandwich	*Un tramezzino*	Oon trametzeeno
A toasted sandwich	*Un toast*	Oon toast

Numbers 1–20

One	*Uno*	Oono
Two	*Due*	Dooay
Three	*Tre*	Tray
Four	*Quattro*	Qwatro
Five	*Cinque*	Chinqway
Six	*Sei*	Sayee
Seven	*Sette*	Settay
Eight	*Otto*	Otto
Nine	*Nove*	Novay
Ten	*Dieci*	Deeaychee
Eleven	*Undici*	Oondeechee
Twelve	*Dodici*	Dohdeechee
Thirteen	*Tredici*	Traydeechee
Fourteen	*Quattordici*	Qwatordeechee
Fifteen	*Quindici*	Qwindeechee
Sixteen	*Sedici*	Saydeechee
Seventeen	*Diciasette*	Deechasettay
Eighteen	*Diciotto*	Deechotto
Nineteen	*Dicianove*	Deechanovay
Twenty	*Venti*	Ventee

Colours

Red	*Rosso*	Rosso
Blue	*Blu*	Bloo
Green	*Verde*	Verday
Yellow	*Giallo*	Jahlow
Brown	*Marrone*	Marohnay
Black	*Nero*	Nero
White	*Bianco*	Beeanco

List of Prayers Used in Text

Glossary

Apostolic See   the basilica is directly answerable to the pope

General Chapter   official gathering of all Franciscans to discuss matters of policy

hagiography   a biography of a saint

host   the consecrated bread of the Eucharist

loggia   arcade with covered top and open sides; a typical feature of medieval Italian houses

lunette   half-moon (or full moon) shape above a door way in the tympanum

majolica   Italian Renaissance enamelled ceramic ware

monstrance   open or transparent receptacle for the consecrated bread (host)

necropolis   large ancient cemetery

tertiary   member of the lay order

tympanum   a triangular space above a door between the lintel and the arch

Vulgate Bible   the Catholic Church's official Latin translation of the Bible

Bibliography

Below are the principal works consulted in writing this book, but various local guides to the sanctuaries and towns were also used.

Marco Bartoli, *Clare of Assisi*, Darton, Longman and Todd 1993

Blue Guide to Umbria, Black Norton 2000

Ian Campbell Ross, *Umbria*, Penguin 1996

Luciano Canonici, *Francis of Assisi*, n.d.

Guide to Assisi, History and Art, Coop Editrice Minerva 1992

Adrian House, *Francis of Assisi*, Chatto and Windus 2000

L'Umbria di Francesco e Chiara, La Voce Edizioni 2000

GianMaria Polidoro, *Francis of Assisi*, Edizioni Porziuncula 1988

William Short, *The Franciscans*, Michael Glazier 1989

Umbria, Touring Club of Italy 1999

Index

The St. Francis Prayer Book

A Guide to Deepen Your Spiritual Life

Jon M. Sweeney

144 pages, Deluxe Paperback
ISBN: 1-55725-352-8, $13.95

This warm-hearted little book is a window into the soul of St. Francis, one of the most passionate and inspiring followers of Jesus. With this guide, readers will:

Pray the words that Francis taught his spiritual brothers and sisters to pray.

Explore Francis' time and place and feel the joy and earnestness of the first Franciscans.

Experience how it is possible to live a contemplative and active life, at the same time.

Available from most booksellers or through Paraclete Press: www.paracletepress.com; 1-800-451-5006.
Try your local bookstore first.